ATARI 130XE MACHINE LANGUAGE FOR THE ABSOLUTE BEGINNER

Kevin Bergin

MELBOURNE HOUSE
PUBLISHERS

First published in the United Kingdom by
Melbourne House (Publishers) Ltd.

This remastered edition
published by
Acorn Books
www.acornbooks.co.uk

This book is a page-by-page reproduction of the original 1985 edition as published by Melbourne House. The entirety of the book is presented with no changes, corrections nor updates to the original text, images and layout; therefore no guarantee is offered as to the accuracy of the information within.

Contents

Foreword

So, you feel you've had enough of BASIC and want to learn more about your machine.

Maybe you use your computer to run some professionally written software, like word processing, accounting systems, educational software or games.

You may have wondered what it is that makes these programs so different from the ones you have written in BASIC. These professional programs seem to be able to do many tasks at the same time, including functions which you may have not realised that your computer can do.

Apart from the size of the programs and the amount of time spent in writing them, the one major difference between your programs and most of the programs that you will buy in a store, is that most professional programs are written wholly or partly in machine language.

Machine language is a must for the really serious programmer. Most games, useful utilities and interfaces are written in machine language.

This book attempts to give you an introduction to the world of machine language, the other side of your 13ØXE.

You will be led through the microprocessor's instruction set slowly at first, practising each instuction learned using the monitor/program entry program ALPA (Assembly Language Programming Aid).

As we work through the instruction set you will meet the new concepts and features of your computer, some of which you may not have known it possessed.

You are encouraged throughout the book to check that the computer's output is what you would logically expect it to be. Keep a pen and paper close at hand to copy on paper what the microprocessor is doing, to get its answers, and to see if your answers agree.

Chapter 1
Introduction to Machine Language

One advantage of machine language (M.L.) is that it allows the
programmer to perform several functions not suited to BASIC.
The most remarkable advantage of machine language, however, is
its speed. On the 13ØXE you can carry out approximately one
hundred thousand M.L instructions per second. BASIC commands
are several hundred times slower.

This is due to the fact that BASIC is written in machine
language and one single BASIC command may be a machine language
program of hundreds of instructions. This is reflected in the
capabilities of each of the languages.

Machine language instructions, as you will see as you work your
way through this book, are extremely limited in what they can
do. They perform only minute tasks and it takes many of them
to achieve any 'useful' function. They perform tasks related
to the actual machinery of the computer. They tell the
computer to remember some numbers and forget others, to see if
a key on the keyboard is pressed, to read and write data to the
cassette tape and to print a character on the screen.

Machine language programs can be thought of as subroutines –
like a subroutine in BASIC – a program within another program
that can be used anywhere in the program and returns to where
it was called from when finished. You use the commands GOSUB
and RETURN to execute and then return from a subroutine.

.
.
.
.

1Ø GOSUB 8ØØØ

.
.
.
.
.

8ØØØ RETURN

1

This wouldn't be a very useful subroutine because it doesn't do anything but it does show how a subroutine works!

Using a machine language program

To call a machine language subroutine from a BASIC program you use the command 'A=USR (address)' where A is a dummy variable. Just as with the GOSUB command you must tell the computer where your routine starts. 'GOSUB 8000' calls the subroutine at line number 8000. Similarly A=USR (8000) calls the machine language subroutine at memory address 8000.

NOTE here that memory address 8000 is very different to line number 8000. A memory address is not a program line number, it is the 'address' of an actual piece of memory in the computer.

Memory addressing

Each piece of memory in the computer can be visualised as a box which can contains one character, one piece of information.

With over 65,000 separate boxes, the computer must have a filing system to keep track of them, so that it can find each separate piece of information when it needs it. The filing system it uses gives each box an 'address', which is like the address of your house. You use addresses to find the one particular house you are looking for anywhere within a busy city. You use this address to visit a house, send it mail or to pick up a parcel from it. The computer, like us, sends information and moves from one place (subroutine) to another using its system of addresses.

The computer's system of addressing is simpler than ours — in its terms, anyway — as it starts at one end of memory and calls this address zero. It then counts through the memory 'boxes', giving each of them a number as it goes — from zero at one end to 65535 right at the other end of memory. For us this would be very difficult to remember, but for the computer it is the logical way to do things. These numbered boxes can be thought of as post office boxes. If you put something in the box at address number one, it will stay there until you replace it with something else.

Each box can hold only one thing at a time. When you put something in a box, what was originally there will be lost forever.

The command 'A=USR (8000)' tells the BASIC to execute a machine language subroutine whose first instruction is stored in the box at address 8000.

Using memory directly from BASIC

There are two other BASIC commands that you will find extremely useful in this work.

They enable us to put things in and collect things from the boxes in memory. These commands are 'PEEK' AND 'POKE'. PRINT PEEK (5ØØ) picks up the contents of the box at memory address 5ØØ and prints it. This can be used like any other function within a BASIC program, e.g. A = PEEK (387) or C = 7*PEEK 1Ø78)+14.

POKE 11ØØ,27 puts the number after the comma, in this case 27, into the box at memory address 11ØØ, e.g. POKE 2179,B or POKE C,X. Try the following:

```
PRINT PEEK (8ØØØ)
POKE 8ØØØ,2ØØ
PRINT PEEK (8ØØØ)
```

We will be using these BASIC commands a lot while experimenting with machine language instructions so that we can find out the result of the programs we write and use. BASIC will be a tool by which we write, run and observe our machine language programs.

Machine language as a subroutine

We have said that our machine language programs will be used like a subroutine in BASIC. In place of the 'GOSUB' we will use the 'USR' command.

In BASIC, as you know, a subroutine must end with the command RETURN.

```
    .
    .
    .
    .
    .
1Ø GOSUB 8ØØØ
    .
    .
    .
    .
    .
8ØØØ ...
    ...
    ...
    ...
8Ø4Ø RETURN
```

3

So too our machine language routines must end with a command to RETURN to the main program but it will not be a BASIC command it will be a machine language instruction.

The machine language instruction for RETURN is 96. That's it, just 96. 96 is what the microprocessor understands as a command to RETURN from a subroutine. It would of course be impossible for us to remember that 96 is return as well as the list of hundreds of other instructions, so we have names for each instruction. These names are meaningless to the computer but, hopefully make some sense to us, the programmers. These names are short simple and to the point, they are called Mnemonics.

One important note here, the USR command allows the user to pass to a machine language program information through parameters. For our purposes we will be passing no parameters. However the 13ØXE always assumes that you are passing at least one parameter and saves the number of parameters in a place called the stack. In our case the number will be zero. This number must be removed from the stack before your machine language program tries to return to BASIC or it will crash the machine. To do this put at the start of your program a PLA, it is 1Ø4 in decimal. If this is impractical then alternatively this instruction can be the second last instruction executed (before the RTS). It is simplest however to make it the first.

The mnemonic for 96 is RTS. RTS stands for RETURN from Subroutine. The mnemonic for 1Ø4 is PLA which stands for Pull accumulator. Where necessary throughout we will provide both the machine code numbers and the mnemonics of an instruction, as this makes it readable to you while at the same time providing the information needed for the computer.

To demonstrate how this works we will create a very short machine language program. Type in the following BASIC lines:

    POKE 8192,1Ø4

    POKE 8193,96

This puts 1Ø4 (the value of PLA instruction) into the memory address of location 8192 and 96 (the value of the RTS instruction) into the box at memory address of location 8193.

Congratulations! You have just created your first machine language program. It doesn't do much; it is just like the empty BASIC subroutine:

4

```
10 GOSUB 8000
8000 RETURN
```

Sitting in the box at memory address 8193 is the instruction 96 (RTS). We will now run (just to check that it works) our program using the command 'USR'. Type in the following BASIC line:

```
A=USR (8192)
```

The computer should respond with READY. It has just executed your program.

Chapter 1 SUMMARY

1. Assembly code is fast. It allows access to the computer's inbuilt hardware functions that are not convenient to use from BASIC.

2. Instructions only perform very simple tasks and so it requires a large number of them to do anything complicated. However each instruction executes very quickly

3. Memory is addressed using numbers from 0 to 65535.

4. A memory address can be thought of as a post office box, which can only hold one piece of information at a time.

5. PEEK is used to examine the contents of a memory location from BASIC.

6. POKE is used to put a number into a memory location from BASIC.

7. USR is used to run a machine language from BASIC.

8. A machine language program called from BASIC must include at least one PLA as the first executable instruction or the second last executable instruction. Please note the difference between the first instruction in a program and the first instruction which is actually executed. They are not the same thing.

9. The value 96 (RTS) must be placed at the end of every machine language program to tell the computer to 'RETURN' from subroutine.

Chapter 2
Basics of Machine Language Programming

Using memory from machine language

So far we have discussed memory, discussed how you can look at things in memory from BASIC, and how to put things in memory from BASIC.

This of course has to be done within our machine language programs as well. We need to be able to pick up some information from one of the boxes in memory, perform operations on it and then return it to the same, or to a different, box in memory. To do this, the microprocessor has devices called registers. These can be thought of as hands which the microprocessor uses to get things done.

The registers

There are three of these hands (registers) called A, X and Y, each of which is suited to a particular range of tasks in the same way that a right handed person uses their right hand to play tennis, their left hand to throw the ball in the air and to serve, and when needed both hands, e.g. to tie their shoes.

These hands (registers) can pick up information from the memory boxes. Like memory they can only hold one piece of information at a time, but they are not themselves a part of the memory as they have no address. They are an actual part of the microprocessor and there are special machine language instructions which deal with each of them seperately.

The accumulator

The first register we will talk about is the 'A' register (or accumulator). As you will see in the following chapters, the accumulator's functions are the most general of the computer's hands. It is also the register which handles most of the microprocessor's mathematical functions.

In most cases, the microprocessor must be holding some
information in one of its hands (registers) before it can do
anything with it. To get the microprocessor to pick up

something from one of the boxes in memory, using the
accumulator, you use the instruction 'LDA'. This mnemonic
stands for load accumulator. This loads the contents of one of
the boxes in memory into the microprocessor's accumulator hand,
e.g.

    LDA 253

This command takes the contents of the box at memory address
253 and puts it in the microprocessor's 'A' hand
(accumulator). The machine code values of this instruction is
165 253.

NOTE here that the machine code is in two parts. Unlike the
command RTS which is in one part, - 96 -, the LDA 253 has one
part for the command LDA, - 165 -, and one part for the address
of the box in memory which contains the information being
picked up, - 253 -. These two parts of the instruction are put
in seperate memory boxes so the boxes containing the program;

```
| LDA 38 |
| RTS    |
```

Would look like:

```
| 165 |
| 38  |
| 96  |
```

Addressing modes

Most machine language instructions have several different forms
or modes, which allow the programmer flexibility in how and
where in memory the data will be put for the program to operate
on. There are eight different forms for LDA alone, called
Addressing Modes.

In various different ways, these addressing modes alter the way
in which the address of the box in memory to be used is
specified within the instruction.

For example, assume you had an instruction to take a letter out
of a certain post office box. Your instructions could tell you
to do this in several different ways:

1. You could be told to look for box number 17.

2. You could be told to look for the box third from the right on the second bottom row.

3. You could be told to look for the box owned by Mr. Smith.

4. You could be told to look for the box whose address was contained in a different box.

5. You could be simply handed the letter.

You will find out more about addressing modes later in the book, but for now you will be introduced to three of the eight different forms of the LDA command.

Mode 1 - 165 253   LDA 253

This is a short form of the LDA. For reasons which will be explained later, it can only access memory over a short range of possible addresses.

Mode 2 - 173 55 4   LDA 1079

This is a longer form of the LDA command; it can access a box anywhere in memory. NOTE here that the machine code is in three parts. The first part - 173 - is the command for LDA in this three part form. The - 55 - and the - 4 - represent the address of the box 1079 which contains the data to be put in the A hand. The reasons for this apparently strange number which makes 1079 into 55,4 will become clear in the following chapter, for now accept it is so. This mode is called absolute addresing.

Mode 3 - 169 71   LDA #71

This command is different from the previous two. Instead of looking for the information to be put into the accumulator in one of the boxes in memory, the information you want is given to you as part of the instruction. In this case the number 71 will be put into the accumulator. It has nothing to do at all with the box at address number 71. Note here that this different type of addressing known as 'immediate' addressing is shown in the mnemonic by a '#' symbol before the number.

We know how to get the microprocessor to pick something up from memory, but before we can do anything useful we have to know how to get the microprocessor to do something with it. To get the microprocessor to place the contents of its A hand (accumulator) in memory, we use the instruction STA which stands for Store accumulator in a specified box in memory.

This instruction too has several addressing modes (seven in fact) but only two of them will be discussed here.

Mode 1 - 133 41   STA 41

This instruction puts the contents of the accumulator in the box at address 41. As in the LDA, the similar instruction in two parts (zero page mode) can only reach a limited number of addresses in memory boxes.

Mode 2 - 141 57 Ø3   STA 825

This is like Mode 1 except that it can put the contents of the accumulator in a box anywhere in memory (absolute addressing). The - 141 - specifies the instruction and the - 57 - and - 3 - contain the address of box 825 (this is explained in Chapter 3).

QUESTION: Why is there no 'STA' immediate mode (see LDA #71)?

ANSWER: The 'immediate' mode in 'LDA #71' puts the number in the instruction - 71 - into the accumulator, somewhat like being handed a letter, not just a post office box number of where to find the letter. STA immediate mode would attempt to put the contents of the accumulator in the STA instruction itself. This is like being told to put a letter not into a post office box but into the instructions you have been given. Obviously this has no practical meaning!

Simple program input

We will now write a few machine language programs to examine the instructions we have learned so far. To make it easier enter the following BASIC program:
    5 PRINT CHR$(125);"...."
    1Ø REM THIS PROGRAM WILL MAKE IT EASIER TO ENTER MACHINE   CODE
PROGRAMS
    2Ø READ A
    3Ø IF A=-1 THEN GOTO 7Ø
    4Ø POKE 1536+X,A
    5Ø X=X+1

10

```
  6Ø GOTO 2Ø
  7Ø PRINT "BEFORE.. -LOCATION 4ØØØØ  ";PEEK (4ØØØØ)
  8Ø Q=USR(1536)
  9Ø PRINT "AFTER...-LOCATION 4ØØØØ  ";PEEK(4ØØØØ)
 1ØØ END
1ØØØ DATA 1Ø4
1Ø1Ø DATA 169,33
1Ø2Ø DATA 141,64,156
1Ø3Ø DATA 96
9999 DATA -1
```

LINES 1ØØØ - 1Ø3Ø contain our machine language program.

LINES 2Ø - 6Ø puts our program from data statements into memory boxes starting from 1536 so it can be executed.

LINES 7Ø - 9Ø print 'BEFORE' and 'AFTER' tests on the memory we are getting our machine language program to change.

When the BASIC program is finished, our machine language program will be contained in memory boxes as follows:

Address	Data
1536	1Ø4
1537	169
1538	33
1539	141
154Ø	64
1541	156
1542	96

For the programmer's benifit this is written out in mnemonic form as follows:

```
1536      PLA
1537      LDA #33
1539      STA 4ØØØØ
1542      RTS
```

Assembly language

A program written out in mnemonic form is called an 'assembly language' program, because to transform this list of letters which can be understood by the programmer into a list of numbers which can be understood by the microprocessor, you use

11

a program called an 'assembler'. Throughout this book we give you programs in mnemonic form e.g. RTS:

address	mnemonics
1536	PLA
1537	LDA #33
1539	STA 40000
1542	RTS

Our BASIC program, as well as placing our machine code in memory, runs our program (see line 80).

You will see by our before and after analysis of memory address 40000 that it has been changed by our program as we intended. The original value of location 40000 could have been anything. The number you see may change each time you run the program. It is impossible to know what will be in memory before you put something in there yourself, just as you can't tell what might be left over in a post office box you haven't looked in before. The value in memory address 40000 after the program has been run is: 33. This shows that your program did what was expected it loaded the number 33 and then stored it into memory at 40000.

Screen memory

There is one result from this program which you may not have expected. Look at the top left hand corner of the screen. You will see it contains an 'A'. Line 5 of the program clears the screen, and nowhere in the BASIC program was the 'A' printed on the screen, therefore it must have been put there by the machine language program. We know the machine language program puts the value 33 into location 40000. Could this print an 'A' on the screen? Try if from BASIC and see what happens. First clear the screen in the normal way and the type:

    POKE 40000,33

You will see that the 'A' has reappeared on the top left hand corner of the screen. This has happened because memory at 40000 has a dual purpose. It is used to display things on the screen, as well as carrying out the remembering functions of normal memory. The post office box description is still valid, but now the boxes seem to have glass fronts so that you can see on your screen what the boxes have inside them. If you look at

12

the table of screen display codes in Appendix 14, you will see that for the value 33 that we placed in location 40000 the character should be displayed is an 'A'.

Let's try to display some of the other characters in the table on the screen. Let's try to print an 'X' on the screen. First we need to look up the table of screen display codes to find the value corresponding to the letter 'X'. You will find that this value is 56. To put this in memory at address 40000 we will use the program we wrote earlier:

```
PLA
LDA #33
STA 40000
RTS
```

But this time we will change LDA #33 to an LDA #56. Using the same BASIC program to put this into memory, we must now change line 1010 which holds the data for the LDA command. This must now read:

```
1010 DATA 169,56:REM LDA #56
```

Our machine language program will now (when the BASIC program is run) read:

```
1536    104          PLA
1537    169 56       LDA #56
1539    141 64 156   STA 40000
1542    96           RTS
```

When this is run you will now see an 'X' appear in the top left hand corner of your screen.

At this stage you might well ask, how do I print something somewhere else on the screen? The answer is simple. 'Screen Memory' (these 'glassfronted' boxes) lives from 40000 all the way through to 40959. It is set up in 24 rows of 40 columns as you see on your screen. Memory at 40000 appears at the top left corner; 40001 appears next to that to the right, and 40002 next to that. Similarly 40000 + 40, 40040 appears immediately under 40000 at the left edge at the second top row and 40040 + 40 (40080) under that, and so on.

Using the same BASIC routine to enter our program, we will now try to print on the row second from the top of the screen. The address of this place on the screen is given by 40000 + 40 (screen base + 1 row) = 40040.

Therefore we want our program to be:

```
PLA          clear the stack of parameter information
LDA #56      Character 'X'
STA 40040    First column second row
RTS
```

To do this we change the data we change the data for our program on line 1020 to read:

```
1020 DATA 141,104,156:REM STA 40040
```

You will also need to alter lines 70 and 90 from 40000 to 40040 before running. The machine language program will now print an 'X' on the second line from the top of the screen.

Printing a message

We will now use our BASIC program to write a bigger machine language program which will display a message on the screen. Type the following lines:

```
1000 DATA 104
1010 DATA 169,40
1020 DATA 141,64,156
1030 DATA 169,37
1040 DATA 141,65,156
1050 DATA 169,44
1060 DATA 141,66,156
1070 DATA 141,67,156
1080 DATA 169,47
1090 DATA 141,68,156
1100 DATA 96
```

Now run the program. You will see that it has printed 'HELLO' at the top of the screen. The machine language program we wrote to do this was:

14

```
Address        MACHINE CODE      ASSEMBLY CODE
1536           1Ø4               PLA          SET UP STACK
1537           169  4Ø           LDA #4Ø      SCREEN CODE FOR 'H'
1539           141  64  156      STA 4ØØØØ
1542           169  37           LDA #37      SCREEN CODE FOR 'E'
1544           141  65  156      STA 4ØØØ1
1547           169  44           LDA #44      SCREEN CODE FOR 'L'
1549           141  66  156      STA 4ØØØ2
1552           141  67  156      STA 4ØØØ3
1555           169  47           LDA #47      SCREEN CODE FOR 'O'
1557           141  68  156      STA 4ØØØ4
156Ø           96                RTS
```

Check the values used with those given in the table of screen
display codes.

It is interesting to note the way in which the two L's were
printed. There was no need to put the value 44 back into the
accumulator after it had been stored in memory once. When you
take something from memory, or when when you put something from
one of the registers (hands) into memory, a copy is taken and
the original remains where it started.

We can write the same programs we have just written using
different addressing modes. It is useful to be able to write
the same program in different ways for reasons of program
efficiency. Sometimes you want a program to be as fast as
possible, sometimes as short as possible, and at other times
you may want it to be understandable and easily debugged.

We will change the program to give us greater flexibility in
what we print. Type in the following lines:

```
      15 PRINT "LETTER VALUE";:INPUT B:POKE 2Ø3,B
  1Ø1Ø DATA 165,2Ø3       :REM LDA 2Ø3
  11ØØ DATA 169,55        :REM LDA #55
  111Ø DATA 141,69,156    :REM STA 4ØØØ5
  112Ø DATA 96            :REM RTS
```

Our machine language program will now look like this:

```
Address        MACHINE CODE      ASSEMBLY CODE
1536           1Ø4               PLA
1537           165  2Ø3          LDA 2Ø3
1539           141  64  156      STA 4ØØØØ
1542           169  37           LDA #37
1544           141  65  156      STA 4ØØØ1
```

15

```
1547                169  44              LDA #44
1549                141  66  156        STA 40002
1552                141  67  156        STA 40003
1555                169  47              LDA #47
1557                141  68  156        STA 40004
1560                169  55              LDA #55
1562                141  69 156          STA 40005
1565                96                   RTS
```

NOTE that this finds its first letter from the box at memory address 203 using zero page addressing instead of immediate addressing. Line 15 of our BASIC program sets this box in memory to be any number we choose. Run this program several times choosing the values, 57,34 and 45.

We have seen in this chapter how memory can have more than one function by the example of the memory between 40000 and 40959, which doubles as screen memory. Similarly other parts of memory can have special functions. Different areas of memory are used to control screen colours, graphics, Player Missile graphics, sound, the keyboard, games controllers (joysticks) and many other I/O (Input/Output) functions. These areas will be referred to throughout the book on a purely introductory level. We encourage you to find more detailed descriptions from more advanced texts.

Chapter 2 SUMMARY

1.   The microprocessor uses registers (like hands) to move data about and work on memory.

2.   It has three general purpose hands; the accumulator, the X register and the Y register.

3.   We use the LDA command to get the microprocessor to pick something up in the accumulator (A hand).

4.   We use the STA command to get the microprocessor to put the contents of the accumulator in to a specified location.

5.   These commands and many others have several different addressing modes which allow us flexibility in the way we store and use our data:

     *   immediate addressing holds the data within the instruction.
        *   absolute addressing uses data stored anywhere in memory.
        *   zero page addressing uses data stored within a limited area of memory.

6. A program written out in mnemonic form is called an assembly language program.

7. Memory is used to display information on the screen.

8. Information is displayed according to a screen display code which gives a numeric value to any printable character.

9. Memory is used to control other I/O (Input/Output) functions of the computer.

Chapter 3
Introduction to Hexadecimal

Uses of hexadecimal

So far in this book we have talked about memory in several different ways, but we have not been specific about what it can and cannot hold. We have used memory to hold numbers which represented characters, numeric values, machine code instructions and memory addresses. We have merely put a number in memory without thinking about how the computer stores it, in all but one case.

It is the absolute addressing mode which has shown us that the computer's numbering system is not as simple as we might of first thought, e.g 141 64 156 is the machine code for STA 40000 , leaving the numbers 64 and 156 signifying the address 40000 . There is obviously something going on which we have not accounted for.

We have previously compared the microprocessor's registers and memory to hands. How big a number can you hold in your hand? Well that depends on what we mean by hold. You can use your fingers to count to five, so you can use one hand to hold a number from zero to five. Does that mean that the biggest number that you can hold is five? You may be surprised to hear that the answer is NO.

Counting from Ø to 5 on your fingers like this

is very wasteful of the resources of your hand, just as counting like that on a computer would be very wasteful of its resources.

Binary

A computer's 'fingers' can either be up or down (on or off, in the same way a light can be on or off) but, as with your fingers, it can tell which of its fingers is on and which is off. In other words, the value represented depends not only on the number of fingers used but also on the position of those fingers. Try this yourself give each finger one of the following values (mark it with a pen if you like).

Now try to count by adding the numbers represented by each finger in the up (on) position:

Try to represent the following numbers on your fingers:

7,16,1∅,21,29

Q. What is the biggest number you can represent on your fingers?
A. 1+2+4+8+16=31

As you can see 31 is quite a significant improvement on 5. The computer's 'hands' are different from ours in several ways. Its fingers are electronic signals which can either be on or off, as opposed to our fingers being up or down. For the programmer's benefit the condition on is given the value 1 and the condition off is given the value ∅.

The other major difference is that the computer has eight 'fingers' on each 'hand'. This may sound silly, but there is no reason for it not to be that way. As it turns out it is a fairly easy set up to handle. The computer's eight fingered hand is called a 'byte' of memory. As with our own fingers, we give each of the computer's 'fingers' one of the following values:

    1,2,4,8,16,32,64,128

Again we count by adding together the values of all those fingers in the 'on' position.

Eight fingered hand	Computer's 'hand' — byte	Number
	0 0 1 1 0 0 0 1	32+16+1 = 49
	1 1 0 0 0 1 0 0	128+64+4 = 196
	0 0 0 1 0 0 0 1	16+1 = 17

Q.   What is the biggest number that can be represented by the computer's 'eight fingered hand'?
A.   128+64+32+16+8+4+2+1=255

Without realising it, what we have done in this chapter is introduce the binary numbering system (base two). All computers work in base two representing electrical on's and off's an endless stream of 1's and 0's. This of course would make the programmer's task of controlling what is going on inside the computer even more confusing than it already is, e.g.:

```
Assembly Code    Machine code    Binary

LDA #33          169  33         10101001 00100001
STA 40000        141  64 156     10001101 01000000 10011100
RTS              96              01100000
```

Why hexadecimal?

This of course would be impossible for a programmer to remember, and difficult to type in correctly. We could of course just use decimal as listed in the machine code column. As it turns out, this is not the most convenient form to use. What we do use is hexadecimal or base sixteen. This may sound strange but it becomes very easy because it relates closely to the actual binary representation stored by the computer.

To convert between binary and hexadecimal is easy. Each hexadecimal digit can store a digit between Ø and 15 (decimal) just as each decimal digit must be between Ø and 9. Therefore one hexadecimal digit represents one half of a byte (eight fingered hand).

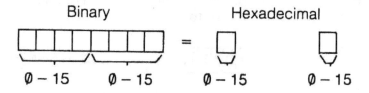

The whole eight fingered hand can be shown by two hexadecimal digits. You might at this point be wondering how one digit can show a number between Ø and 15. Well it is exactly the same as decimal the numbers 1Ø, 11, 12, 13, 14, 15 (decimal) are represented by the letters A, B, C, D, E, F respectively.

BINARY	DECIMAL	HEXADECIMAL
ØØØØ	Ø	Ø
ØØØ1	1	1
ØØ1Ø	2	2
ØØ11	3	3
Ø1ØØ	4	4
Ø1Ø1	5	5
Ø11Ø	6	6
Ø111	7	7
1ØØØ	8	8
1ØØ1	9	9
1Ø1Ø	1Ø	A
1Ø11	11	B
11ØØ	12	C
11Ø1	13	D
111Ø	14	E
1111	15	F
1ØØØØ	16	1Ø

This shows that converting from binary to hexadecimal is merely dividing into easy-to-see segments of four (fingers).

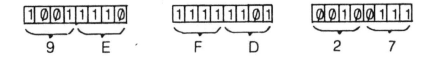

Hex and Binary mathematically

Mathematically any base, 1Ø, 2, 16 or 179 follows a simple format. Each digit takes the value Ax (BASE) Position -1

In other words in decimal 98617 is

$7 \times 10^0 + 1 \times 10^1 + 6 \times 10^2 + 8 \times 10^3 + 9 \times 10^4$ = 98617
$7 \times 1 + 1 \times 1Ø + 6 \times 100 + 8 \times 1000 + 9 \times 10000$ = 98617
$7 + 1Ø + 6ØØ + 8ØØØ + 9ØØØØ$ = 98617

In binary Ø1Ø11101 is

$1 \times 2^0 + Ø \times 2^1 + 1 \times 2^2 + 1 \times 2^3 + 1 \times 2^4 + Ø \times 2^5 + 1 \times 2^6 + Ø \times 2^7 = 93$
$1 \times 1 + Ø \times 2 + 1 \times 4 + 1 \times 8 + 1 \times 16 + Ø \times 32 + 1 \times 64 + Ø \times 128 = 93$
$1 + Ø + 4 + 8 + 16 + Ø + 64 + Ø$ = 93

In hexadecimal A7C4E is

$14 \times 16^0 + 4 \times 16^1 + 12 \times 16^2 + 7 \times 16^3 + 1Ø \times 16^4$ = 687182
$14 \times 1 + 4 \times 16 + 12 \times 256 + 7 \times 4Ø96 + 1Ø \times 65536$ = 687182
$14 + 64 + 3Ø72 + 28672 + 655360$ = 687182

Several points should be noted here. Firstly, any number which can be stored in one memory box, (a number from Ø to 255) can be stored in 8 binary digits (bits), or as we have been calling them till now 'fingers'. Any number from Ø to 255 can also fit in two hexadecimal digits (FF = 15 x 16 + 15 x 1 = 255).

This, however, is where our problem with absolute addressing occurs. If we can't put a number bigger than 255 into memory, how do we specify an address which may be between Ø and 65535 (64K)? The solution is to use two boxes, not added together but as part of the same number. When dealing with addresses we are dealing with 16 finger (16 bit) (2 byte) binary numbers. This is the same as saying four digit hexadecimal numbers. The largest number we can hold in a four digit hexadecimal number is:

```
FFFF = 15 x 1 + 15 x 16 + 15 x 256 + 15 x 4Ø96
     = 15 + 24Ø + 384Ø + 6144Ø
     = 65535 = 64K
```

which is large enough to address all of memory, e.g., the 2 byte (16 bit) hex number 13A9 equals:

```
    1           3           A           9
  ØØØ1        ØØ11        1Ø1Ø        1ØØ1

  (((1 x 16) +3) *256) + (1Ø x 16 + 9)
  = 4864+169
  = 5Ø33
```

For example, the two byte hex number Ø4Ø5

```
  = 4 x 256 + 5
  = 1Ø24 + 5
  = 1Ø29
```

Absolute addressing

If you look back at the beginning of this chapter you will see that this is the problem associated with absolute addressing which we have been able to solve. One other thing to remember with absolute addressing is that the bytes of the address are always backwards, e.g.,

```
  STA 4ØØØØ
  141 64 156
```

The most significant byte (high byte) – 156 is placed last, and the least significant byte (low byte) – 64 is placed first. NOTE that this is the reverse of normal storage, e.g., normally 17 where 1 is the most significant digit (1 x 1Ø) is stored first. The 7 (7 x 1) is the least significant and comes second. The bytes of an absolute address are always stored low byte, high byte.

This chapter also explains zero page addressing. Two byte instructions leave only one byte to specify the address, e.g., LDA 38 – 165 38. We have said before that when using 1 byte we can only count from Ø to 255. Therefore zero page addressing

24

can only address the first 256 bytes of memory. A block of 256 bytes is called a 'page'.

To specify the fact that we are using hexadecimal this book follows the standard practice of placing a $ sign before a hexadecimal number.

```
LDA 40000    is the same as   LDA $9C40
LDA 65535    is the same as   LDA $FFFF
LDA 0        is the same as   LDA $0
```

From now on all machine code listings will also be shown in hexadecimal;

address	code			mnemonics
1536	68			PLA
1537	A9	21		LDA #$21
1539	8D	40	9C	STA $9C40
1542	60			RTS

irrespective of the format used in the assembly code, which will vary depending on the application.

Converting hexadecimal to decimal

We have provided a table in appendix 3 for quick hexadecimal to decimal conversions. To use this chart for single byte numbers, look up the vertical columns for the first hexadecimal (hex) digit and the horizontal rows for the second digit e.g.;

```
$2A - 3rd row down
      11th column from left
Printed there is  LO    HI
                  42    10752
```

Look at the number under LO (low byte). 42 is decimal for $2A hex. For 2 byte hex numbers divide into 2 single bytes. For the left byte (or high byte) look up under HI and add to the low byte e.g.;

```
$7156      divide HI = $71  LO = $56
HI - 71 - 8th row down
          2nd column left
```

```
LO    HI
113   28928
```

```
LO - 56 - 6th row down
          7th column from left
```

```
LO    HI
86    22016
```

Add high and low 28928 + 86 = 29014
$7156 = 29014

```
NOTE:  in all cases    LO    HI
                       X     Y
```

$$Y = 256 * X$$

The high byte is 256 times value of the same low byte.

Chapter 3 SUMMARY

1.   In counting on a computer's 'fingers', position (which fingers), as well as the number of fingers, is important.

2.   Each of the computer's hands and each piece of memory has 8 'fingers', and the biggest number they can hold in each is 255

3.   An eight 'fingered' piece of memory is called a byte.

4.   Each finger has a value which depends on its position. The fingers are numbered from zero to seven and their possible values are 1,2,4,8,16,32,64 and 128.

5.   Hexadecimal (base sixteen) is the grouping together of binary. 1 Hex digit = 4 binary digits. Hex is easier to handle than binary or decimal.

6.   DECIMAL 0 1 2 3 4 5 6 7 8 9 10 11 12 13 14 15 16 17 18
      HEX   0 1 2 3 4 5 6 7 8 9 A B C D E F 10 11 12

7.   Zero page addressing can access the first 256 bytes, the maximum addressable by one byte.

8.   Absolute addressing can access 65536 (64K) bytes of memory
(all), which is the maximum addressable by 2 bytes.

9.   Absolute addresses are always stored low byte first then
high byte, e.g., 8D 98 17   LDA $1798.

1Ø. Hexadecimal numbers are specified by prefixing them with a
$ sign.

11. Remember the quick conversion table for hex to decimal in
Appendix 3.

Chapter 4
Introduction to ALPA +
Disassembler

We have provided you with two BASIC programs to help you put
your machine language programs into memory. The first program
is called ALPA which is an acronym for 'Assembly Language
Programming Aid'. A listing of this program appears in
Appendix 11. We have also provided a disassembler program to
examine the ROMs and your programs. A listing of this can be
found in Appendix 11 as well. In Chapter 2 we used a small
BASIC program to put our machine language programs into memory,
but as you can imagine, it would very soon become a tiresome
process if we had to use this method every time when we wanted
to enter our programs. Throughout the rest of the book we have
given all our examples of machine language programs in ALPA
format. The features of ALPA are:

1. Programs are stored as text and can be edited with commands
like INSERT, DELETE and APPEND. Text is converted into machine
language by giving the ASM command. This command assembles
your program and put the resulting code into an array called
MEM. Thus assembling your program will not crash the machine.

2. The programs you write with the editor can be saved or
loaded to disk or tape. So you can work on a program, save it
to tape, go away and reload it later.

3. To help in inserting, deleting and editing, each
instruction is put on a seperate line with a line number which
you can use to reference it. The linenumber is generated
automatically by the line editor.

4. The program can be listed using the LIST command and
stopped with the CTRL and '1' keys.

5. A line is divided into three fields. Field one contains
the label, field two the operation code and field three the
operand. Each of the fields are reached by pressing the TAB
key - except in the case of field one, where the cursor is
placed at the required position by the computer. After a line
is typed and RETURN is pressed a new line number will appear

29

automatically. Pressing RETURN at the start of a blank line will take you back to the command mode.

6. Your program can be stored anywhere in memory by using the ORG instruction at the beginning of the program. The ORG instruction uses four digit hexadecimal characters only.

7. Instead of referencing a memory location with an absolute address it is possible to specify a label. So instead of using $4567 it's possible to define $4567 as a label and just use the label. An exception to this rule is the branch instruction. The destination specified in branch instructions must have an ampersand before the label name or before the absolute address specification.

```
e.g. TABLE   NOP
             NOP
             JMP     TABLE
             LDA     TABLE,X
             BNE     &LABEL
             BNE     &$0028
```

8. There are four assembler directives available in ALPA. These are not actually 6502 instructions but commands to the assembler which are imbedded in the listing. They are ORG, EQU, DFB and DFW.

ORG — used to set the point in memory where programs are to be assembled (it sets the program counter). An ORG statement expects a four digit hexadecimal number following ORG and any thing else will cause an illegal hexadecimal number error. Only one ORG statement is permitted in a program. ORG also defines the execution address of a program for the RUN command.

```
e.g.     ORG $0005
```

EQU — assigns a value to a label. It is possible to assign a zero page value or absolute value to a label.

```
e.g.     LABEL   EQU     $0005
         ONE     EQU     $12
```

DFB —generates a byte of data from a hexadecimal value ($00 – $FF) supplied and puts it in the program at the current program counter location. There can only be one hexadecimal byte per DFB instruction.

```
e.g.     DFB     $12
```

DFW —generates a word of data from a hexadecimal value, splits it into two bytes and puts the two bytes into the

30

current program counter location and the next one. Its also automatically reverses the order of the bytes. Therefore if you give the assembler the value $FF11, then the bytes generated will not be put in memory in the order $FF and $11 but $11 and $FF.
  e.g.   DFW $FA9Ø

To get ALPA running

A Listing of ALPA appears in Appendix 11.

1. Type in the program exactly as it has been listed in Appendix 11.

2. When you have finished typing it in, save ALPA immediately (for cassette save type: SAVE "C:ALPA" for disk save type: SAVE"D:ALPA")

NOTE:
1. If you have made an error while typing in a line then the ATARI will reject it and print an error message. The error message will be inserted in the actual program line, so it will be necessary to retype the entire line or use the cursor editing keys to remove it.

2. Even though a line may be accepted when it was entered, it is still possible for it to contain errors. For example, the ATARI cannot tell if a variable name is wrong, because the names of variables are chosen by the programmer (e.g. VAR$="A" instead of VAS$="A" would not be detected as an error by the computer, but would result in an error report when the program was RUN). So if ALPA does not work, carefully compare what you have typed in with the ALPA listing in the book.

Using ALPA

All numbers used in ALPA are to be entered in hexadecimal. Zero page hex numbers are distinguished from absolute hex numbers by their length. Zero page numbers are expected to be two digits long and absolute numbers four digits long.

When ALPA is first initialised it is, by default, in Command mode. An asterisk and cursor will appear and ALPA will be waiting for a command. To enter the text editor use the command 'APPEND'. This will put you in the editor at the next line number, this will be '1' if there is no text. At this stage you are ready to type in your program. The programs you will write will be in the following format:

31

linenumber Label   Operation-Code   Operand.   (seperated
into fields with the TAB key).

        - operation code is the mnemonic instruction of the
command you want to type. Followed by the operand (e.g.
address or data), as in the following:

    1 LABEL   LDA #$Ø5

    or

    1   STA $9C4Ø

ALPA commands

The following commands are available in ALPA:

1. LIST
This command will display a range of linenumbers. Type LIST
and press RETURN. It will ask for the starting linenumber and
the ending linenumber.

2. ASM
This command assembles your source program into an array and
all references are resolved according to the value of the PC.
NOTE you must ASM a program before you can RUN it.

3. RUN
This command executes your program in memory starting from the
first address specified by the ORG statement. It does this by
copying the machine code in the array MEM into memory and then
calling the program with USR. The ASM command must be used
prior to the RUN command.

4. WATCH
This command asks you which address you want to 'WATCH' and
invokes the WATCH function. The contents of the address
specified will be printed before and after the program in
memory is executed by RUN. This is used to observe the results
of a program on memory.

5. NWATCH
This command turns off the WATCH feature.

6. LOAD
This command loads an ALPA program saved using the SAVE command
in ALPA from cassette or disk. Type LOAD and press RETURN, a
prompt will appear and you must enter the device to load the

program from and the filename. No quotes are necessary round the filename.

7. SAVE
This command saves the current ALPA program to cassette or disk for LOADing in the future to work on without having to type it in again. It works in the same fashion as LOAD.

8. DELETE
This command deletes a line from the program. Type DELETE and press RETURN, then input the linenumber you want deleted.

9. INSERT
This command allows you to insert lines into the text. Lines are inserted after the line number specified. The command takes the form:

    INSERT (Press RETURN)
    :linenumber (Press RETURN)

Then enter the text as usual. This mode is exited by pressing RETURN at the start of a new line.

10. QUIT
This command exits ALPA and returns you to BASIC. It is possible to restart ALPA with GOTO 12.

11. NEW
Removes your program from the text buffer (Deletes all of the text).

Memory usage in ALPA

You will notice that we have, consistently throughout the book, used only a few areas of memory for our programs and our data. We have not done this because they are the only ones that will work, but because we tried to use memory that we are sure that nobody else (BASIC, the Operating Sytem and ALPA itself) will be using.

The programs that run within the computer all the time, BASIC and the Operating System, use specific areas of memory to store their own data in. It is good programming practice to know and avoid these areas to ensure that your program does not stop the Operating Sytem or BASIC from functioning properly. (Remember ALPA is written in BASIC). By checking through the memory maps and memory usage charts provided in Appendices 6 and 8, you

33

will be able to find other areas to use, but throughout the book we have mainly used memory at:

    $0600 - $06FF
    $CB   - $CF zero page

The best areas to use in zero page memory, when it is very full, are areas set as aside as buffers etc.

If a program written in machine code looks as if it is never going to stop, it may well not. One way to stop these programs is to press RESET. You will be put back into BASIC with the usual screen display. If this does not work then the machine is well and truly 'hung' and nothing short of switching off and on will reset the machine.

To continue in ALPA with your program intact, type GOTO 12 (unless you switched off). This is also the procedure to follow if you accidentally leave ALPA. If this does not work type RUN. This should get ALPA working again, but your program will be lost.

We will now repeat some of the programs we used earlier, to demonstrate the use of ALPA, e.g.,

```
              PLA
              LDA #$21
              STA $9C40
              RTS
```

This is the program we used at the beginning of chapter 2. To use ALPA, testing location $9C40 (40000) before and after the program, type the instructions on the right hand side of the program above, e.g.,

```
1              ORG $0600
2              PLA
3              LDA #$21
4              STA $9C40
5              RTS
```

The computer will print the next line number and wait for input. After you have typed in the program, assemble it with the ASM command. To watch the change in location $9C40 type:
    WATCH
    To which the computer will reply:
    (what address)? $9C40

34

Now execute the program with the RUN command and study the output before and after the program was executed. Type NEW to remove the program and try out some of the other programs in chapter 2 using ALPA. Remember that ALPA uses only hex numbers and that Chapter 2 uses decimal, so it will be necessary to convert from decimal to hex.

Further use of ALPA will be discussed as it becomes relevant to the commands being discussed.

There is a disassembler to accompany ALPA. It is listed in Appendix 11 along with the listing ALPA. After the disassembler has been successfully typed in and saved, it can be used to disassemble memory and examine various parts of the 130XE. It can also be used to disassemble your programs. To do this the object code must be in an area that will not be overwritten by the disassembler, if this is so you can load and run the disassembler. The Disassembler supports the following commands.

1. MEM
This command asks you the question 'DISASSEMBLE FROM WHAT ADDRESS:?' It will then disassemble (produce assembly code) using the contents of memory from the address specified for one screen. Any key except E will produce another screen of disassembly. Press the E key to exit to normal command mode.

2. DUM
This command asks you the question 'DUMP MEMORY FROM WHAT ADDRESS:?' It will then produce a 'hex dump' of memory from that address as a series of hex bytes.

3. EXI
Using this command will exit the dissasembler and pass control back to BASIC.

4. ASC
Displays an area of memory in ASCII character format.

5. CMD
Displays a list of the disassemblers commands.

Chapter 4 SUMMARY

1. We will use ALPA to enter all of our machine language programs after this Chapter.

2. ALPA's commands are as follows:

   APPEND
   LIST
   RUN
   WATCH
   NWATCH
   LOAD
   SAVE
   DELETE
   INSERT
   QUIT
   NEW

3. Although we will list programs in the form:
    line ###   Instructions   in   Assembly   Language,   you   need
only type the instructions and leave the rest up to ALPA.

4. The Disassembler has the following commands:

   MEM
   DUM
   CMD
   EXI
   ASC

Chapter 5
Microprocessor Equipment

In the previous four chapters we have covered a lot of the groundwork needed to understand the intricacies of machine code programming. More of the basics will be introduced as we go along. We have covered enough at this stage to move on to such things as using machine language to do some arithmetic.

Storing numbers

We know from Chapter 3 that the largest number we can store in a single byte (memory location) is 255. We have also seen that for addresses bigger than 255 we could use 2 bytes to represent them in low byte/high byte format so that Address = low byte + 256 x high byte.

Surely then we could use the same method to represent any sort of number greater than 255 and less than 65536 (65535 = 255 + 256 x 255), and in fact if necessary this can be taken even further to represent even higher numbers.

Numb = 1st byte + 256 x 2nd byte + 65536 x 3rd byte + ...etc

The carry flag

Now, when we add two 1 byte numbers together it is possible that the result is going to be larger than 255. What then can we do with the result of the addition? If we put the result in one byte it could be no bigger than 255, so:

2Ø7 + 194 = 4Ø1 mod 256 = 145

but also

58 + 87 = 145

Surely there is something wrong here. We must somehow be able to store the extra information lost when a result is larger than 255. There is provision for this within the 6502 microprocessor in the form of a single bit (single finger) 'flag' called the carry flag. The carry flag is 'set' (turned on) if a result is geater than 255, e.g.,

```
207 + 194 = 145;  carry = 1
58  + 87  = 145;  carry = 0
```

NOTE: a single bit is large enough to cover all possible cases of carry.

```
  11111111              255
+ 11111111            + 255

1 11111110 + carry    254 + carry
```

Therefore to add 2 byte numbers together, you add the low bytes first and store the result, and then and the high bytes including the carry bit from the addition of the low bytes, e.g.,

```
30A7 + 2CC4 = 5D6B
```

is done in the following manner:

```
    low bytes

    A7
 +  C4
    6B        carry set

    high bytes

    30
 +  2C
 +   1        carry bit

    5D

    Answer = 5D6B
```

38

Adding numbers

To handle this, the machine language instruction to add two 1 byte numbers together is ADC (add with carry). This adds the specified number (or memory) plus carry flag to the accumulator and leaves the result in the accumulator.

The instruction automatically adds in the carry bit to its calculation. Therefore since the carry could be set before you put anything in it (like memory – see chapter 1), it is necessary to set the carry to zero before an addition if that addition does not want to add the carry of a previous calculation. To set the carry flag to zero we use the instruction CLC (Clear Carry Flag) before such ADC's.

Type in the following program, using ALPA:

```
NEW
APPEND
1                    ORG $0600
2                    PLA
3                    LDA #$03
4                    CLC
5                    ADC #$05
6                    STA $03FD
7                    RTS

WATCH
(watch address )? 03FD
ASM
RUN
```

The program will print:

```
'address 03FD before' = 00      3
'address 03FD after'  = 08     +5
                               ‾‾
                                8
```

We will now change lines 3 and 5 to alter the sum we are performing. NEW the old program and replace it with:

```
1                    ORG $0600
2                    PLA
3                    LDA #$27
4                    CLC
5                    ADC #$F4
6                    STA $03FD
7                    RTS
```

ASM and RUN the program and the computer will respond with:


```
        address Ø3FD before = Ø8
        address Ø3FD after  = 1B


                    27
                  + F4
carry is set      1 1B
```


NOTE: we cannot tell the carry has been set from our results.

We will now change the program again. This time we will deliberately set the carry using SEC (Set Carry Flag) command before doing our addition. Remove the last program with NEW and type the following lines:

```
1                       ORG $Ø6ØØ
2                       PLA
3                       LDA #$Ø3
4                       SEC
5                       ADC #$Ø5
6                       STA $Ø3FD
7                       RTS
```

ASM and RUN the program, and the computer will respond with:

```
        address Ø3FD before = 1B
        address Ø3FD after  = Ø9
```


```
          3
        + 5
        + 1        (carry bit)
        = 9
```


Type in the following lines:

```
1                       ORG $Ø6ØØ
2                       PLA
3                       LDA #$27
4                       CLC
5                       ADC #$F4
6                       LDA #$Ø3 ·
7                       ADC #$14
8                       STA $Ø3FD
9                       RTS
```

ASM and RUN the program.

```
address Ø3FD before = Ø9
address Ø3FD after  = 18
```

The carry is set by the addition on line 5 and carries through
to the second addition on line 7, hence:

```
            27              3
          + F4            + 14
Carry =    1 1B          +  1   (carry)
                         = 18
```

Now change line 5 and repeat

```
    1                    ORG  $Ø6ØØ
    2                    PLA
    3                    LDA  #$27
    4                    CLC
    5                    ADC  #$2Ø
    6                    LDA  #$Ø3
    7                    ADC  #$14
    8                    STA  $Ø3FD
    9                    RTS
```

```
address Ø3FD before = 18
address Ø3FD after  = 17
```

```
              27              3
            + 2Ø            + 14
carry Ø  =   47            +  Ø   (carry)
                          = 17
```

From these we see how the carry bit is carried along with the
result of one addition to another.

We will now use this to do an addition of 2 byte numbers using
the method we described previously.

Two Byte addition

Suppose we want to add the numbers 6C67 and 49B2.

```
    6C67
  + 49B2

  = ????
```

41

To do this we must separate the problem into two single byte additions:

```
low bytes      67      high bytes     6C
             + B2                    + 49
                        carry        +  1
carry  =    1 19
                                       B6
```

Clear the previous program using the NEW command and then type the following:

```
1                      ORG $Ø6ØØ
2                      PLA
3                      LDA #$67
4                      CLC
5                      ADC #$B2
6                      STA $Ø3FD
7                      LDA #$6C
8                      ADC #$49
9                      STA $Ø3FE
1Ø                     RTS
```

This will store the low byte of the result in Ø3FD and the high byte of the result in Ø3FE. To check our answer we will use the WATCH command on both bytes (by running twice).

```
ASM and RUN the program
address Ø3FD before = ??
address Ø3FD after  = 19
```

Now type:

```
WATCH
(watch address )? Ø3FE
RUN
address before = ??
address after  = B6
```

Now join the high byte and the low byte of the result to give the answer:

```
  6C67
+ 49B2

  B619
```

This procedure can be extended to add numbers of any length of bytes.

Subtracting numbers

The microprocessor, as well as having an add command has a subtract command. Similar to the ADC command the SBC (Subtract with Carry) uses the carry flag in its calculations. Because of the way in which the microprocessor does the subtraction, the carry bit is inverted (1 becomes Ø and Ø becomes 1) in the calculation, therefore

```
    8              8
  - 5            - 5
  - 1            - CARRY  (CARRY = 1)

  = 2            = 3
```

Consequently, to do a subtraction without carry, the carry flag must be set to 1 before the SBC command is used. Remove the previous program and type the following:

```
1              ORG $Ø6ØØ
2              PLA
3              LDA #$Ø8
4              CLC
5              SBC #$Ø5
6              STA $Ø3FD
7              RTS
```

WATCH
(watch address)? Ø3FD
ASM and RUN this program.

You will see from the results that by clearing the carry instead of setting it has given us the wrong answer. We will now correct our mistake by setting the carry to 1 before the subtract. Replace the previous program with this one:

```
1              ORG $Ø6ØØ
2              PLA
3              LDA #$Ø8
4              SEC
5              SBC #$Ø5
6              STA $Ø3FD
7              RTS
```

ASM and RUN

43

You will now see that we have the correct answer:

```
        8                8
      - 5              - 5
(CARRY Ø)  - 1         - Ø   (CARRY = 1)

      = 2              = 3
```

You may have wondered how the microprocessor handles subtractions where the result is less than zero. Try for example 8 − E = − 6. Change line 5 of the program, ASM and RUN it.

```
1                    ORG $Ø6ØØ
2                    PLA
3                    LDA #$Ø8
4                    SEC
5                    SBC #$ØE
6                    STA $Ø3FD
7                    RTS
```

address Ø3FD before = ??
address Ø3FD after = FA

```
        8      or    BORROW = 1Ø8 carry cleared to zero
      - E                    - E

      - 6                     FA
```

NOTE: that − 6 = Ø − 6 = FA
            FA + 6 = Ø

This clearing of the carry to signify a borrow can be used for multibyte subtraction in the same way as it can for multibyte addition. Try to write a program to do the following subtraction:

$E615 − $7198

Here is an example

```
1                    ORG $Ø6ØØ
2                    PLA
```

44

```
3                    LDA #$15
4                    SEC
5                    SBC #$98
6                    STA $Ø3FD
7                    LDA #$E6
8                    SBC #$71
9                    STA $Ø3FE
1Ø                   RTS
```

ASM and RUN this, noting the results. Use WATCH to observe
$3FE — the high byte of the result and RUN again. Combine the
high and low bytes of the result to get the answer $747D.

These instructions ADC and SBC can be used in many addressing
modes, like most other instructions. In this chapter we have
only used immediate addressing.

NOTE: SEC and CLC have only one addressing mode — implied.
They perform a set/reset on a specific bit of the status
register and there are no alternative addressing modes. Their
method of addressing is 'implied' within the instruction.

An exercise

Write a program to add the value $37 to the contents of memory
location $Ø3FD using ADC in the 'absolute' addressing mode, and
put the result back there. Use WATCH to observe the results.

```
NOTE here:

LDA #$FF
CLC
ADC #$Ø1
```

leaves the value #$ØØ in A with the carry set, and

```
LDA #$ØØ
SEC
SBC #$Ø1
```

leaves the value #$FF in A with the carry clear (borrow).

Therefore we have what is called 'wrap-around'. Counting up
past 255 will start again from Ø, and counting down past zero
will count from 255 down.

45

Chapter 5 SUMMARY

1. Any size number may be represented by using more than 1 byte. Numb = 1st byte + 2nd byte x 256 + 3rd byte x 65536 + ...etc.

2. The 6502 microprocessor has a carry flag which is set to signify the carry of data into the high byte of a two byte addition.

3. ADC adds two bytes plus the contents of the carry flag. A CLC should be used if the carry is irrelevant to the addition.

4. ADC sets the carry flag if the result is greater than 255, and clears it if it is not. The answer left in the accumulator is always less than 256. (A = Result Mod 256).

5. SBC subtracts memory from the accumulator and then subtracts the inverse of the carry flag. So as not to have the carry interfere with the calculations, a SEC should be used before SBC.

6. SBC sets the carry flag if the result does not require a borrow (A - M > 0). The carry flag is cleared if (A - M < 0) and the result left in A is 256 - (A - M).

7. Two byte addition:

        CLEAR CARRY
        XX = ADD LOW BYTES + (CARRY = 0)
        YY = ADD HIGH BYTES + (CARRY = ?)
        Result is $YYXX

8. Two byte subtraction:

        SET CARRY
        XX = SUBTRACT LOW BYTES - INVERSE (CARRY = 1)
        YY = SUBTRACT HIGH BYTES - INVERSE CARRY (CARRY = ?)
        Result is $YYXX

Chapter 6
Program Control

Player-Missile Graphics

Back in Chapter 2 we saw how we could display information on the screen by placing that data in 'screen memory'. There is a special 'chip' in the Atari 130XE which handles screen oriented tasks. It is called the Antic-chip. (A brief guide appears in Appendix 5). Using the techniques of addition and subtraction that we learned in the previous chapter, we will look at some of the following features available on the ANTIC chip.

Type in the following program using ALPA:

```
NEW
NWATCH
APPEND
1               ORG $0600
2               PLA
3               LDA #$03
4               STA $D01D
5               LDA #$3E
6               STA $022F
7               LDA #$01
8               STA $D008
9               LDA #$32
10              STA $D000
11              LDA #$58
12              STA $02C0
13              LDA #$90
14              STA $6A
15              STA $D407
16              LDA #$02
17              STA $9432
18              LDA #$E2
19              STA $9433
20              LDA #$42
21              STA $9434
22              STA $9435
```

47

```
23                          LDA #$FF
24                          STA $9436
25                          RTS
ASM and RUN.
```

This should produce a small space ship near the top left of the
screen. This square is known as a 'Player Missile Graphics'.
It is the size of eight double sized pixels but can be moved
about the screen quite easily and over other characters. It is
controlled by the registers (hands) of the ANTIC chip. These
registers are similar to the registers of the microprocessor
but in order to use them directly they have been 'mapped' onto
memory from D400 to D5FF.

The term 'mapped' means that these registers have been put over
the memory. When you access the memory you are in fact dealing
with the registers of the ANTIC chip or whatever else may be
mapped over that memory. To use the description of the post
office boxes we were using before, you could imagine this sort
of mapped memory as post office boxes with false bottoms, and
chutes that connect the box to some sort of machine somewhere
else in the post office.

Moving Player-Missile Graphics

What we are going to do is write a program to move our Player
around the screen. The horizontal position of the four players
is controlled by registers at locations 53248 to 53251. We are
going to move player zero across the screen by incrementing his
horizontal position register (53248).

Looping using JMP

There is an instruction for this — it is the JMP (JUMP)
instruction. Like BASIC's 'GOTO' you have to tell the 'JMP'
where to jump to in the form JMP address (JMP low Low Byte,
High Byte) (ABSOLUTE ADDRESSING).

We will use this instruction to create a program equivalent to
the following BASIC program.

    INITIALISE

    100 POKE 53248,X:X=X+4
    110 GOTO 100

48
```
```

Delete the RTS from the end of the last program and add the following lines with APPEND:

```
26  LOOP       LDX COUNT
27             INX
28             INX
29             INX
30             INX
31             STX $D000
32             STX COUNT
33             JMP LOOP
34  COUNT      DFB $00
```

ALPA label name addressing

The addressing mode used in line 33 is absolute addressing. One of ALPA's features is that it will calculate addresses for you. Normally, when using JMP in absolute addressing mode, you would have to work out the address you want the JMP command to go to - which can be a nuisance as shown in the following samples:

```
1.  0600:  4C 08 06    JMP $0608
    0603:  A9 02       LDA #$02
    0605:  8D FD 03    STA $3FD
    0608:  60          RTS


2.  03FF:  4C FD 03    JMP $03FD
    0402:  A9 02       LDA #$02
    0404:  8D FD 03    STA $03FD
    0407:  60          RTS


3.  0600:  4C 0B 06    JMP $060B
    0603:  A9 02       LDA #$02
    0605:  18          CLC
    0606:  69 04       ADC #$04
    0608:  8D FD 03    STA $3FD
    060B:  60          RTS
```

To create program 2. from program 1.

In other words to move the same program to a different part of memory, you would have to go through the whole program, each time changing all the JMP instructions that JMP to an address within the program, and change them (and only them) to point to a new address.

49

To create program 3. from program 1.

This is done by the addition of a few short commands, something you might often do while debugging. You would also have to change any JMP commands to a new address. This would of course be extremely frustrating, time consuming and error prone. Therefore ALPA has a facility for specifying the address of the JMP as a label. When the program is entered into memory with ASM, ALPA converts the reference from a label to an absolute address which the microprocessor can understand and execute.You can see these addresses being generated when the ASM command is given.

You will notice that the PMG (Player missile Graphic) is moving across the screen at speeds that make it blur completely. This is only a small indication of the speed of a machine code program.

Infinite loops

You will also notice that the program is still going. Just like the program

```
1ØØ POKE 53248,X:X=X+4
11Ø GOTO 1ØØ
```

Our program will go forever around the loop we have created. This is called being stuck in an 'infinite loop'.

The 'BREAK' key will not get us out of this loop. There is a machine code program which is part of BASIC that tests to see if the BREAK key was pressed, but our program does not look at the keyboard. There are only two ways to escape from an infinite loop. One is to press the 'SYSTEM RESET key, which creates an NMI (Non Maskable Interrupt) which will stop the computer and return it to BASIC. The other way to stop the program is to turn the computer off. Press the SYSTEM RESET key and you will be returned to BASIC, to continue in ALPA with your program intact type:

```
GOTO 12
```

There is no other way to exit a machine language routine unless it returns by itself using an RTS. Type LIST. NOTE that because of the JMP the program would never gets as far as an RTS, as in the following BASIC program:

```
10 X=4
20 PRINT "HELLO";X
30 X=X+4
40 GOTO 20
50 END
```

Obviously the END statement is never reached here, because of the GOTO in line 40.

To get this program to print HELLO 4 to HELLO 100 we would write:

```
10 X=4
20 PRINT "HELLO";X
30 X=X+4
40 IF X=104 GOTO 60
50 GOTO 20
60 END
```

Here line 40 will GOTO line 60 only if X=104 and the program will GOTO the END statement and stop. If X is not equal to 104, the program will GOTO line 50 and continue around the loop to line 20. To do this in machine language we need one instruction to compare two numbers (X and 104) and another instruction to JMP depending on the result of the comparison (IF .... GOTO 60).

Comparing numbers

We have previously (see Chapter 5) met the idea of a flag. It is a single bit (single finger) value held inside the microprocessor. In chapter 5 we met the carry flag which was set to signify the need for a carry in a multibyte addition (reset or cleared for a borrow in multibyte subtraction). The microprocessor has seven flags for different purposes which it keeps in a special purpose register called the Processor Status Code Register (or Status Byte).
These seven flags (and one blank) are each represented by their own bit (finger) within this byte and have special microprocessor commands dealing with them. These flags are set

or reset by most machine code commands. (More will be said about them in Chapter 1∅). For example, ADC sets or resets the carry flag depending on the result of the addition. Similarly 'CMP' (Compare), which compares the contents of the accumulator with the contents of a memory location (depending on the addressing mode), signifies its result by setting or resetting flags in the status byte.

Branch instructions

The other instructions we said we would need to write our program is one which would jump dependant on the values of the processor status flags. This form of instruction is called a 'branch' instruction. It is different from the JMP instruction not only in the fact that it is conditional (dependant on the conditions of the status flags), but it is unique in that it uses the relative addressing mode.

Relative addressing means that the address used is calculated relative to the branch instruction. More will be said about relative addressing and the way the branch instructions work at the end of this chapter. Meanwhile we will use ALPA to calculate the address for us as we did with the JMP instruction.

Zero Flag

To test if the result of a CMP instruction on two numbers is equal we use the BEQ (Branch on Equal) command.

To add this to our previous machine language program DELETE the last nine lines of the previous program and replace them with these, using APPEND:

```
25  LOOP        LDA COUNT
26              CMP #$78
27              BEQ EXIT
28              CLC
29              ADC #$∅1
3∅              STA $D∅∅∅
31              STA COUNT
32              JMP LOOP
33  EXIT        RTS
34  COUNT       DFB $∅∅
```

52

Line 3Ø has been changed so that the Player does not move as far in each jump, hence the the player will be slowed down. Also a different method of incrementing the horizontal position has been used. Despite incrementing the horizontal position register by only one pixel, it will still be moving too fast to be seen. ASM and RUN this program.

NOTE: ALPA has calculated and 'OK'ed both addresses using the label references.

You will see this time that the player moved about halfway across the screen and stopped as the program ended normally with an RTS.

Program summary

Lines 1 −24	Initialisation
Lines 25–32	Player movement loop
Line 27	Test for end condition
Line 33	end

We have managed to find a way to use a loop that tests for a condition on which to exit a loop. We could however make this more efficient by creating a program that looped until a certain condition was met. This difference is subtle but it is shown by this BASIC program in comparision to the previous one.

```
1Ø X=4
2Ø PRINT "HELLO";X
3Ø X=X+4
4Ø IF X<>1Ø4 THEN 2Ø
5Ø END
```

By creating a loop until a condition is reached we have saved ourselves one line of the program. If speed or space were important to the program, this would be a useful alteration. Overall it is good programming practice to write code with these considerations in mind. It produces neater, less tangled programs that are easier to read and debug.

This programming method translates well into machine language using the BNE (Branch on Not Equal) command.

Delete the last ten lines of the previous program and add these to the end of it with APPEND:

```
25  LOOP        LDA COUNT
26              CLC
27              ADC #$Ø1
28              STA $DØØØ
29              CMP #$8Ø
3Ø              BNE &LOOP
31              RTS
32  COUNT       DFB $ØØ
```

LIST the program as it currently stands.

Program summary

Lines 1 −24	Initialisation
Lines 25−3Ø	Player movement loop
Lines 31	end

You will see that by changing the loop we have untangled the flow of the program. ASM and RUN the program to verify that it still functions the same with the changes. As you can see, there are many ways to write the same program. The notion of right and wrong ways of machine language programming are absurd, to quote a well used phrase, 'Don't knock it if it works'. It may be that programs that are structured well are better for you as they are more legible and easier to understand.

There is a lot we can learn by knowing how an instruction works. The CMP instruction for example compares two numbers by doing a subtraction (accumulator − memory) without storing the result in the accumulator. Only the status flags are set or reset. They in fact test the status register 'zero' flag and stand for:

BEQ − Branch on Equal to zero
BNE − Branch on Not Equal to zero

It is the condition of the zero flag which is set by the result of the subtraction done by the CMP command (accumulator − memory = Ø which sets the zero flag = 1). This flag is then tested by the BEQ or BNE command. This may seem a meaningless point until you realise that, since the CMP command is done by subtraction, the carry flag will also be set by the result. In other words, if the subtraction perfomed by the CMP needs a 'borrow' (A − Mem < Ø, A less than memory), then the carry will be cleared (CARRY = Ø). If the subtraction does not need a 'borrow' (A − Mem > Ø, A greater than or equal to memory), then the carry will be set (CARRY =1)

Therefore the CMP command tests not only A = Mem but also A <
Mem and A < Mem and therefore (if A > Mem but A <> Mem) then A
> Mem. We can now write our BASIC program:


```
1Ø X=4
2Ø PRINT "HELLO";X
3Ø X=X+4
4Ø IF X<1Ø1 GOTO 2Ø
5Ø END
```


This makes the program even more self explanatory. It shows
clearly that values of X bigger than the cutoff 1ØØ will not be
printed. To test for the accumulator less than memory, you use
the CMP followed by BCC (Branch on Carry Clear) because a
borrow will have occurred. To test for the accumulator greater
than or equal to memory use CMP followed by BCS (branch on
Carry Set).

Write a machine language program to move a player across the
screen and test for A < memory (as in previous BASIC programs).

Relative addressing

All branch instructions using an address mode called relative
addressing (JMP is not a branch instruction). In relative
addressing the address (the destination of the branch) is
calculated relative to the branch instruction. All branch
instructions are two bytes long – one byte specifies the
instruction the other byte specifies the address. This works
by the second byte specifying an offset to the address of the
first byte after the instruction according to the Tables in
Appendix 4. From Ø – 7F means and equivalent branch forward
and from 8Ø – FF means a branch backward of 256 – the value.

Therefore:

```
     FØ Ø3      BEQ dest
     8D FD Ø3   STA $3FD
dest 6Ø         RTS
```

will be the same no matter where in memory it is placed.

The value 3 as part of the branch instruction is the number of
bytes to the beginning of the next instruction (8D).

```
1st next byte (ØØ)
2nd next byte (Ø6)
3rd next byte (6Ø)
```

With the following programs, check that the destination address of the branch is in fact the address of instruction after the branch plus the offset, e.g,

```
0600: FO 03          BEQ $0605
0602: 8D FD 03        STA $3FD
0605: 60              RTS
```

and

```
03FD: FO 03           BEQ $0402
03FF: 8D 00 06         STA $600
0402: 60               RTS
```

The machine code remains the same but the disassembled version differs. The program will work exactly the same at either address. This is completely opposite to the case of the JMP which uses absolute addressing and cannot be relocated. Fortunately we do not have to calculate offsets using the tables, because these offsets would have to be recalculated every time we added an instruction between the branch command and its destination address. When we use the branch command we can get ALPA to calculate the offset for us using branch label name.

Use ALPA to write some programs with branch instructions in them, using the label feature, and check ALPA's output by disassembling the ASMed code, then verify that the branch takes the correct path using the relative branch table in Appendix 4.

Chapter 6 SUMMARY

1. A Player-Missile is a character eight pixels wide ,256 pixels high and the size of 32 normal characters, which can be moved over the screen on top or behind other characters.

2. The command JMP address is the equivalent to BASIC's GOTO command. It makes the program jump to the address specified.

3. ALPA can handle addresses as either absolute addresses ($5610) or as labels, e.g, JMP WORD (Jump to the value of the label WORD).

4. To break out of an infinite loop, press system RESET and to start ALPA without losing your current program enter: GOTO 12

5. The microprocessor's STATUS CODE Register has seven flags (and one blank) which are set by some machine code instructions.

6. Branch instructions jump conditional on the state of the flag referred to by the instruction, e.g.,

```
BEQ Branch on Equal         Z = 1
BNE Branch on Not Equal     Z = Ø
BCS Branch on Carry Set     C = 1
BCC Branch on Carry Clear   C = Ø
```

7. The CMP compares two bytes (by doing a subtraction without storing the results). Only the flags are set by the outcome.

Flags	CARRY	ZERO	Signifies
	Ø	Ø	A < Mem
Value	1	1	A = Mem
	1	Ø	A > Mem
	1	?	A >= Mem

8. Relative addressing mode, used only for branch instructions, specifies an address relative to the instruction which uses it, e.g. BNE Ø3 means branch three memory addresses forward (see table Appendix 4). The destination of a branch instruction is preceeded by an ampersand which tells the assembler that the addressing mode is relative.

9. ALPA handles this addressing for you if you specify branch labels.

Chapter 7
Counting, Looping and Pointing

Counting to control a loop

Suppose we want to multiply two numbers together. There is no
single machine language instruction which can do this, so we
would have to write a program to do it. We could for example,
add one number to a total as many times as the other number is
large. e.g,

```
10 A=7
20 T=T+A:REM add three times
30 T=T+A
40 T=T+A
50 PRINT "7*3=";T
```

It would be much easier and more practical (especially for
large numbers) to do this in a loop. e.g.,

```
10 A=7:B=3
20 T=T+A
30 B=B-1
40 IF B<>0 THEN GOTO 20
50 PRINT "7*3=";T
```

NOTE: this is by no means the best way to multiply two numbers,
but we are only interested in the instructions here. A
preferred method is described in chapter 10.

Counting using the accumulator

In this short program, unlike any other program we have dealt
with previously, there are two variables. A, which we are
adding to the total, and B which controls the loop. In this

case we couldn't stop our loop as we have done in the past by
testing the total, because we would have to know the answer
before we could write the program. Our machine language
program would look, along the lines of what we have done
previously, like this:

```
 1              ORG $Ø6ØØ
 2              PLA
 3              LDA #$ØØ
 4              STA A
 5              LDA #$Ø3
 6              STA B
 7   LOOP       LDA A
 8              CLC
 9              ADC #$Ø7
1Ø              STA A
11              LDA B
12              SEC
13              SBC #$Ø1
14              STA B
15              BNE &LOOP
16              RTS
17 A            DFB $ØØ
18 B            DFB $ØØ
```

Counting using memory

Most of this program consists of loading and storing between
the accumulator and memory. Since we so often seem to be
adding or subtracting the number one from a value as a counter,
or for other reasons, there are special commands to do this for
us. INC (Increment Memory) increments the contents of the
address specified by one and puts the result back in memory at
the same address. The same goes for DEC (Decrement Memory),
except that it subtracts 1 from memory.

NOTE: INC and DEC do not set the carry flag – they do set the
zero flag.

We will now write the program thus:

```
    NEW
    APPEND

    1              ORG $Ø6ØØ
    2              PLA
```

```
3                      LDA  #$Ø3
4                      STA  $Ø3FD
5                      LDA  #$ØØ
6   LOOP               CLC
7                      ADC  #$Ø7
8                      DEC  $Ø3FD
9                      BNE  &LOOP
1Ø                     STA  $Ø3FE
11                     RTS
```

Program summary

Line 2   Balance stack
Line 3 - 5   Initialise
Line 6 - 9   Loop until result of DEC = Ø
Line 1Ø-11   end

Using INC or DEC we can use any memory location as a counter, leaving the accumulator free to do other things.

An exercise

Rewrite the previous progam using INC and CMP to test for the end of the loop.

The X and Y registers

There are however even easier ways to create counters than using INC and DEC. Looking back to Chapter 2, we mentioned that the 65Ø2 microprocessor had three general purpose registers – A, X and Y. Then for the last few chapters we have been talking solely of the most general purpose register, the accumulator. So, you may now ask, what are the other 'hands' of the microprocessor, the X and Y registers for?

and what does 'general purpose' mean? Well, so far we have met one non-general-purpose register, the microprocessor status register (there are another two which we will meet in future chapters). The status byte can only be used to contain status flags and nothing else, as compared to the accumulator which can hold any number between Ø and 255 representing anything.

The X and Y can, like the accumulator, hold any number between Ø and 255, but there are many functions of the accumulator they

61

cannot do, e.g., Addition or Subtraction. The X and Y registers are extremely useful as counters.

They can perform the following operations (compared to those we have already discussed for the accumulator and for memory).

LDA	Load Accumulator with memory
LDX	Load X with memory
LDY	Load Y with memory
STA	Store Accumulator in memory
STX	Store X in memory
STY	Store Y in memory
INC	Increment memory
INX	Increment X (Implied addressing mode)
INY	Increment Y
DEC	Decrement memory
DEX	Decrement X (Implied adressing mode)
DEY	Decrement Y
CMP	Compare Accumulator with memory
CPX	Compare X with memory
CPY	Compare Y with memory

Using the X register as a counter

We will now write our multiplication program using the X register as the counter. Type in the following:

```
NEW
WATCH
(WHAT ADDRESS )? Ø3FD
APPEND

1                    ORG $Ø6ØØ
2                    PLA
3                    LDX #$Ø3
4                    LDA #$ØØ
5    LOOP            CLC
6                    ADC #$Ø7
7                    DEX
8                    BNE &LOOP
9                    STA $Ø3FD
1Ø                   RTS
```

62

This routine is slightly shorter and considerably faster than the orginal but otherwise not all that different. Rewrite all the commands using the X register and replace them with the equivalent Y register commands. Practise using the X and Y register in place of or with the accumulator in some of our previous programs.

Moving blocks of memory

How would you write a program to move a block of memory from one place to another? For instance to move the memory from 8000 - $8050 to the memory at $7000 - $7050. The following is how not to do it:

```
        LDA $8000
        STA $7000
        LDA $8001
        STA $7001
        LDA $8002
           .
           .
           .
```

etc.

This is a ridiculous way to even think of moving blocks of memory, because of the size of the program we would have to create (However it is the absolute fastest method of moving blocks of memory).

One possible way of writing the program would be:

```
        LDA $8000
        STA $7000
```

followed by some code which did a two byte increment to the address part of the instruction and then a loop to go through the whole block to be moved. This is an extremley interesting concept to think about. It is a program which changes itself as it functions, it is called 'self modifying code'.

But because it changes itself it is very hard to use correctly. It is also considered very poor programming practice to use because it is prone to errors (one mistake in writing or calculations will send your computer crazy and you will probably have to switch off and back on to recover). Self modifying code is also extremely hard to debug. However, there can be some advantages, it would be very hard for anyone to understand this kind of coding (protection) and it may be safe to use if carefully written and well documented.

Self modifying code is therefore obviously not the answer to our problem. The answer in fact, lies in addressing modes. Originally we called addressing modes ways of accessing data and memory in different formats. We have so far seen:

Implied addressing

The data is specified as part of the instruction, e.g., SEC, DEY.

Relative addressing

Addressing relative to the instruction – used only in branches.

Absolute addressing

The data is specified by a two byte address in low byte, high byte format.

Indexed addressing

Our new method of addressing is called 'indexed addressing'. It finds the data to be used by adding a byte index to the absolute address specified in the instruction. The indexing byte is taken from the X or Y register (depending on the instruction used). The X and Y registers are called 'Index registers'.

To use our post office analogy, it is like being given two pieces of paper, one with a two byte address on it and one with a one byte index ($\emptyset$ - 255). To find the correct box you must add the two numbers together to obtain the correct result. The number on the indexing paper may have been changed, the next time you are asked to do this.

Using the X register as an Index

With this addressing mode, our program to move a block of data becomes quite simple. Type the following:

```
     NEW
     APPEND


     1                    ORG $Ø6ØØ
     2                    PLA
     3                    LDX #$ØØ
     4     LOOP           LDA $9C4Ø,X
     5                    STA $9C68,X
     6                    INX
     7                    CPX #$28
     8                    BNE &LOOP
     9                    RTS
```

NOTE here that the mnemonic form of indexed addressing has its
address field made up by the absolute address, a comma and the
register used as the index, even though the following is true:

```
     BD4Ø9C               LDA $9C4Ø,X
     B94Ø9C               LDA $9C4Ø,Y
```

It is the instruction, not the address field, which changes in
the actual machine code. RUN the program. As you can see, we
have used the screen memory again to show that we have in fact
duplicated a block of memory. One line on the screen will be
copied into the line below (the first line onto the second
line). Be sure to have some text on the first line to see the
effect!

Non-symmetry of commands

If, as was suggested when we introduced the X and Y registers,
you have substituted the X or Y for the accumulator in some of
the early programs, you may be wondering if we could do that
here. The answer is no. Not all the commands can use all the
addressing modes. Neither Y or X (obviously not X) can use the
index, X addressing mode being used here with the store (STA).
It is possible to do a LDY ADDR,X but not a STY ADDR,X.   For a
list of addressing modes possible for each instruction, don't
forget Appendix 1.

Searching through memory

We can use the knowledge we have gained up to this point to
achieve some interesting tasks quite simply.   For example, if

asked to find the fourth occurrence of a certain number, e.g., A9 within 255 bytes of given address, how do we do it?

The best way is to start simply and work your way up. To find the first occurrence of A9 we could write:

```
        NEW
        APPEND

        1                       ORG $Ø6ØØ
        2                       PLA
        3                       LDY #$ØØ
        4    LOOP               LDA #$A9
        5                       CMP $FØØØ,Y
        6                       BEQ &FOUND
        7                       INY
        8                       BNE &LOOP
        9                       RTS (not having found A9 from FØØØ -
FØFF)
        1Ø   FOUND              RTS (having found an A9)
```

We would put a counter program around this routine:

```
                LDX #$ØØ
countloop       FIND 'A9'
                INX
                CPX #$Ø4
                BNE countloop
```

We can combine these into a single program:

```
        1                       ORG $Ø6ØØ
        2                       PLA
        3                       LDX #$ØØ
        4                       LDY #$ØØ
        5                       LDA #$A9
        6    LOOP1              CMP $FØØØ,Y
        7                       BEQ &LOOP3
        8    LOOP2              INY
        9                       BNE &LØØP1
        1Ø                      STX $Ø3FD
        11                      RTS
        12   LOOP3              INX
        13                      CPX #$Ø4
        14                      BNE &LOOP2
        15                      STX $Ø3FD
        16                      RTS
```

In this program, when finished, if X = 4, then the fourth occurence of A9 was at $F000,Y (through RTS at line 16).

If X < 4, there were not four occurrences of A9 from $F000 to $F0FF (through RTS at line 11)

Line 14 continues the find routine from the 'INY'. If it started from the 'CMP' it would still be looking at the A9 found before. Type:

```
WATCH
(What address )? 03FD
```

ASM and RUN this program. The results will tell you whether four A9's were found. Change the program to tell you where the fourth A9 was located (STY $03FD). ASM and RUN it again to see the result. We will now change a few things to make this program clearer (as in the earlier chapter). Type the following:

```
NEW
APPEND
```

```
1                   ORG $0600
2                   PLA
3                   LDX #$00
4                   LDY #$00
5                   LDA #$A9
6    LOOP           INY
7                   BEQ &EXIT
8                   CMP $EFFF,Y
9                   BNE &LOOP
10                  INX
11                  CPX #$04
12                  BNE &LOOP
13                  STX $033D
14   EXIT          RTS
```

As shown before this program should now be easier to follow. Type:

Program Summary

Lines 1 – 5	Initialisation
Lines 6 – 9	Find 'A9' loop
Lines 10–12	Counter
Lines 13–14	End

(Since Y is incremented before it is used, its initial index value is 1. Therefore the compare instruction address field has been set back by 1.)

67

ASM and RUN the program. The WATCH function will show you the results the contents of $03FD = contents of X = number of 'A9's' found. (The maximum is still 4 – you can change this in line 11 if you wish).

Using more than one Index

We will now write a program using both index registers to index different data at the same time. Our program will create a list of all the numbers lower than $38 from $F000 to $F0FF. Type the following:

```
NEW
APPEND

1               ORG $0600
2               PLA
3               LDX #$00
4               LDY #$FF
5    LOOP       INY
6               LDA $F000,Y
7               CMP #$38
8               BCS &LOOP2
9               STA $9C40,X
10              INX
11 LOOP2        CPY #$FF
12              BNE &LOOP
13              STX $03FD
14              RTS

WATCH
(what address )? 03FD
```

X here is used as a pointer (index) to where we are storing our results. Y is used as a pointer to where we are reading our data from. NOTE here that Y starts at $FF, and is incremented so at the first $A9 the Y register contains zero.

To test for numbers less than $38 we have used CMP and BCS (A >= Mem see Chapter 6) to skip the store and increment the storage pointer instructions. ASM and RUN the program.

Zero page indexed addressing

All the indexing instructions we have used so far have been indexed from an absolute address (absolute indexed addressing).

68

It is also possible to index from a zero page address (see chapter 2). To rewrite the previous program to look through the first 256 bytes of memory (∅ - 255), all we need to do is change line 4∅ to LDA $∅∅,Y. But if you check with the list of instructions in Appendix 1, there is no 'LDA zero page,Y' - only 'LDA zero page,X'. We have two choices of what to do here. In practice we would probably continue using the absolute indexed instruction.

```
BD ∅∅∅∅                    LDA $∅∅∅∅,Y
```

For the purposes of this exercise, however, we will swap all the usages of X and Y and use the LDA zero page,X. Type:

```
NEW
APPEND

1                          ORG $∅6∅∅
2                          PLA
3                          LDY #$∅∅
4                          LDX #$FF
5    LOOP                  INX
6                          LDA $∅∅,X
7                          CMP #$38
8                          BCS &LOOP1
9                          STA $9C4∅,Y
1∅                         INY
11 LOOP1                   CPX #$FF
12                         BNE &LOOP
13                         STY $∅334
14                         RTS

LIST

ASM and RUN
```

This shows that you must be careful with your choice of registers. Although they can do many of the same things, there are some commands which cannot be done by some registers in some addressing modes. It is wise to constantly refer to the list of instructions in Appendix 1 while writing programs.

Chapter 7 SUMMARY

1. INC - adds one to the contents of memory at the specified address.

2. DEC – subtracts one from the contents of memory at the address specified.

3. The zero flag (but not the carry) is set by the INC and DEC instructions.

4. These are mostly used as loop counters to keep the accumulator free for other things.

5. X and Y the microprocessor's other two general purpose registers (the first being the accumulator), can be used as counters or as index registers.

6. Indexed addressing adds the value of the register specified to the absolute (or zero page) address used to calculate the final address of the data to be used.

7. Many of the instructions are similar if used on A, X or Y, but there are certain instructions and addressing modes which are not available for each register. When writing programs, make sure the instructions you are trying to use exist in the format you wish to use them in!

Chapter 8
Using Information Stored in Tables

One of the major uses of index registers is the looking up of tables. Tables may be used for many reasons – to hold data, to hold addresses of various subroutines, or perhaps to aid in the complex conversion of data from one form to another.

Displaying characters as graphics

One such conversion, for which there is no formula that can be used, is the conversion from screen code to the shape of the character displayed on the screen. Normally this done by the computer's hardware and we do not have to worry about it. When we are in graphics mode, however, this part of the computer's hardware is turned off. In normal character screen mode, our post office boxes within screen memory display through their 'glass' fronts the character which corresponds to the number stored in that box.

That is, we are seeing what is in the box through some sort of 'filter' which converts each number into a different shape to display on the screen. In graphics mode, this 'filter' is taken away and what we see is each bit (finger) of each number stored throughout screen memory. For each bit in each byte that is turned on, there is a dot (pixel) on the screen.

In other words the byte $11 which looks like '00010001' would be displayed on the screen as eight dots, three black dots followed by one white dot, followed by three black dots, followed by one white dot. Depending on your television, you may be able to see the dots making up the characters on your screen. Each character is made up by a grid of eight dots wide and eight dots high. Since we have just determined that we can display eight dots on the screen using one byte, it follows that to display one character eight dots wide by eight dots high, we would need to use eight bytes one on top of the next.

For example a character would look like:

8 x 8 pixel grid	binary byte equivalent	hexadecimal byte equivalent

	binary	hex
0	00011000	18
1	00100100	24
2	01000010	42
3	01111110	7E
4	01000010	42
5	01000010	42
6	01000010	42
7	00000000	0

Graphics memory

The memory as displayed in graphics mode 8 runs straight across the screen. Each byte represents eight pixels horizontally and there is 40 bytes to a row. In the character mode we saw that the screen memory started at $9C40, $9C41 next to that, $9C42 next to that and so on to the end of the first row. In graphics mode 8 the characters are displayed as follows; the top left hand corner of the screen is at $8150, $8151 is directly opposite and $8177 is at the end of the line. The next row of pixels down start at $8178 ($8150+$28), the next row down at $81A0 ($8150+$50) and so on down to the end of graphic memory at $9F4F.

In this way the screen memory is defined one line block at a time (forty bytes horizontally) across the screen. This is the same for all 192 rows positions down the screen. This means there can be forty bytes by eight bits (40 x 8 = 320 pixels) across the screen.

$8150	$8151				$8176	$8177
$8178	$8179				$819E	$819F
$81A0	$81A1					$81C7
$81C8						$81EF
$81FO						$8217
$8218			320			$823F
$8240						$8267
$8268			192			$828F

$9F4D	$9F4E	$9F4F

72

The entire screen in graphics mode 8 is 320 x 192 pixels and takes up 320 x 192 / 8 = 7680 bytes of memory (this is for a full graphics mode not a mixed text and graphics). The starting point of the screen in both graphics and character mode can be changed to suit the programmer (see Appendix 6). It is possible to see the BASIC program ALPA on the screen as a series of dots. It is vitally important that we do not overwrite ALPA while drawing on the screen.

We have shown that the shape of the character A can be represented by a string of eight bytes. We have also shown that the first eight bytes of screen memory make up one character position. Therefore by putting those eight values into those eight bytes, we could make an A appear on the screen in the top left hand corner.

Copying the character sets from ROM

Type in the following program. It will copy some of the character sets down from character memory to where they can be more easily used. Don't worry about the instructions here not yet covered. Executing this program as it presently stands won't change anything.

```
        NEW
        APPEND
1                       ORG $0600
2                       PLA
3                       LDA #$00
4                       STA $CB
5                       STA $CD
6                       LDA #$90
7                       STA $CC
8                       LDA #$E0
9                       STA $CD
10  LOOP1               LDY #$00
11  LOOP2               LDA ($CD),Y
12                      STA ($CB),Y
13                      INY
14                      BNE &LOOP2
15                      INC $CC
16                      INC $CE
17                      LDA $CE
18                      CMP #$E3
19                      BNE &LOOP1
20                      RTS

        NWATCH
        ASM and RUN this program.
```

73

You now have a copy of the ROM character set starting at RAM memory location $9ØØØ. Only the first 128 characters have been copied by this routine.

We will now add to the end of the last program to define our own characters. At the moment there is a copy of the characters in RAM but the video chip is still fetching it's character definitions from ROM. We must tell the video chip to start getting it's definitions from RAM. To do this we load memory location 756 decimal with the page of the character set. A page in 65Ø2 is defined as 256 bytes. The definitions in RAM can then be changed to suit us. Add these lines to the end of your last program. Delete the last line from your program and Type:

```
        APPEND

        2Ø              LDA #$9Ø
        21              STA #$Ø2F4
        22              LDA #$FF
        23              STA $9ØØØ
        24              STA $9ØØ1
        25              STA $9ØØ2
        26              STA $9ØØ3
        27              STA $9ØØ4
        28              STA $9ØØ5
        29              STA $9ØØ6
        3Ø              STA $9ØØ7
        31              RTS
```

ASM and RUN this program.

We now have our character set starting at $9ØØØ and our space has been redefined as a solid block of pixels. To put back the orginal character set press RESET and GOTO 12. The RESET routine replaces the pointer to the ROM routine.

Indirect indexed addressing

There will be some cases where you may be unsure as to which table you want to find your data in. In other words, imagine a program which lets you decide whether you wanted to print the message in upper or lower case letters after the program had run. You will want to use one of the two tables decided on midway through the program. This could be done by two nearly identical programs, each accessing a different table in memory and have the beginning of the program decide which one to use. Of course, this would be wasteful of memory.

To access data using this method, there is an addressing mode called indirect indexed addressing, which allows you even greater flexibility as to where you place your data. Indirect indexed addressing is similar to absolute indexed addressing except that the absolute address is not part of the instruction but is held in two successive zero page locations pointed to by the indirect indexed instruction. In other words, the contents of the zero page address pointed to by the indirect indexed instruction, is the low byte (of a low byte – high byte pair) that contains an address which is indexed by the index register Y to obtain the final address. (Indirect indexed addressing is always indexed using the 'Y' register).

Imagine the following situation using our post office box analogy. You are handed an instruction to look in a box (zero page). The number you find in that box and the box next to it, go together to make an absolute address (low byte – high byte format). You are then told to add an index (Y) to this address to find the address you are looking for.

The mnemonic for this instruction is QQQ (ZP),Y where QQQ is an instruction of the form, LDA. ZP is a one byte zero page address and the Y is outside the bracket to signify that the indirection is taken first, and the index added later. Type in the following example program:

```
NEW
APPEND
1                       ORG $0600
2                       PLA
3                       LDA #$00
4                       STA $CB
5                       LDA #$E0
6                       STA $CC
7                       LDA #$40
8                       STA $CD
9                       LDA #$9C
10                      STA $CE
11                      JSR COPY

12                      LDA #$00
13                      STA $CB
14                      LDA #$E1
15                      STA $CC
16                      JSR WAIT
17                      JSR COPY
18                      RTS
19      COPY            LDY #$00
20                      LDX #$FF
21      COPYA           LDA ($CB),Y
22                      STA ($CD),Y
```

75

```
23                    INY
24                    DEX
25                    BNE &COPYA
26                    RTS
27   WAIT             LDY #$FF
28   WAITA            LDX #$FF
29   WAITB            DEX
3Ø                    NOP
31                    NOP
32                    BNE &WAITB
33                    DEY
34                    BNE &WAITA
35                    RTS
```

This program will copy part of the ROM data to the screen, wait for a second and then copy some other ROM data to the screen. The subroutine COPY will move any page to any other page. It is only necessary to change the pointer to the souce in $CB-$CC and the pointer to the destination in $CD-$CE and call the routine. The beauty of indirect Y is that it can make a subroutine totally generalized. By just changing some zero page locations, pointers are changed and a subroutine can use totally different data. The instruction NOP doesn't do anything, it just takes a certain amount of time to execute and is used as a time delay.

To change the data that is being displayed change the source pointers on lines 3,5,12 and 14. Needless to say the indirect Y instruction is incredibly useful, however it must be used with discretion. There are only 256 zero page memory locations.

Register transfer instructions

In the last program we used an instruction that you haven't previously met – TAY (Transfer A into Y). This is only one of a group of quite simple instructions to transfer the contents of one register to another.

The available instructions are:

```
TAX        (Transfer A into X)
TAY        (Transfer A into Y

TXA        (Transfer X into A)
TYA        (Transfer Y into A)
```

76

These instructions are used mainly when the operations performed on a counter or index require mathematical manipulations that must be done in the accumulator and then returned to the index register.

NOTE:there is no instruction to transfer between X and Y. If necessary this must be done through A.

There are two addressing modes that we have not yet covered which we will briefly touch on here. The first is called Indexed Indirect addressing. No, it is not the one we have just covered, that was the Indirect Indexed addressing. The order of the words explains the order of the operations. Previously we saw indirect indexed in the form, QQQ (ZP),Y, where the indirection was performed first followed by the indexing.

In indexed indirect QQQ (ZP,X), the indexing is done first to calculate the zero page address which contains the first byte of a two byte address (low byte – high byte format), this is the eventual destination of the instruction.

Imagine that you had a table of addresses in zero page. These addresses point to data or seperate tables in memory. To find the first byte of these tables you would use this instruction to index through the zero page table and use the correct address to find the data from the table you were looking for. In terms of post office boxes, we are saying here is the number of a post office box (zero page). Add to that address the value of the indexing byte (X register). From that calculated address, and from the box next to it (low byte – high byte), we create the address which we will use to locate the data we want to work on.

Indirect addressing

The last addressing mode we will cover is called Indirect absolute addressing. There is only one instruction which uses indirect addressing and that is the JMP command.

The JMP using absolute addressing 'Jumps' the program to the address specified in the instruction (like GOTO in BASIC).

In indirect addressing, 'JMP (address)', the two byte (absolute) address within the brackets is used to point to an address anywhere in memory that holds the low byte of a two byte address, which is the destination of the instruction. In other words, the instruction points to an address that, with the next address in memory, specifies the destination of the Jump. In post office box terms, this means that you are handed the number of a box. You look at the box and the one next to it to piece together (low byte - high byte format) the address that the JMP instruction will use.

The major use of this instruction is known as vectored input or output. For example if you write a program that jumps directly to the ROM output character address to print a character, and then you wish output to be directed to disk, you would have to change the JMP instruction. Using the vectored output, the program does a JMP indirect on a RAM memory location. If the disk operating system is told to take control of output, it sets up the vector locations so a JMP indirect will go to its programs. If output is directed to the screen those locations will hold the address of the ROM printing routines, and your program will output through there.

Below is a list of the addressing modes available on the 6502 microprocessor.

	Implied	QQQ
	Absolute	QQQ addr
	Zero Page	QQQ ZP
	Immediate	QQQ #byte
	Relative	BQQ Byte - (L# from ALPA)
	Absolute,X	QQQ addr,X
	Absolute,Y	QQQ addr,Y
Indexed		
	Zero Page,X	QQQ ZP,X
	Zero Page,Y	QQQ ZP,Y
	Indirect Indexed	QQQ (ZP),Y
	Indexed Indirect	QQQ (ZP,X)
	Indirect	JMP (addr)
also		
	Accumulator	QQQ A

(An operation performed on the accumulator, see Chapter 10).

Chapter 8 SUMMARY

1. In graphics mode 0 the screen is organized as 24 lines of 40 characters. Each line is organized as a sequential portion of memory.

2. Characters are defined within an 8 x 8 pixel grid.

3. Screen memory in graphics mode 8 runs across the screen in lines of bytes and then down the screen row by row.

4. The normal character set is stored in ROM at $EØØØ, but can be copied to RAM and altered.

5. Index registers are used to look up tables (among other things), using several indexed addressing modes.

6. In normal indexed addressing, the index register is added to an absolute (or zero page) address to calculate the destination address.

7. In indirect indexed addressing, the destination address is calculated by adding the contents of the Y register to to the 2 byte address stored in zero page locations pointed to by the one byte address in the instruction.

8. In indexed indirect addressing, the eventual address is calculated by adding the X register to the zero page address which forms part of the instruction.

9. TAX, TAY, TXA and TYA are used to transfer data between the index registers and the accumulator.

1Ø. Indirect absolute addressing is for JMP only and uses the contents of two bytes (next to each other), anywhere in memory, as the destination address for the jump.

Chapter 9
Processor Status Codes

We mentioned in Chapters 5 and 6 the concept of flags within the microprocessor. We talked about the carry flag and the zero flag, and we discussed the branch instructions and other instructions associated with them, e.g., SEC, CLC, BCS, BCS, BEQ and BCC. We said that these flags along with several others, were stored in a special purpose register within the microprocessor called the processor status code register or, simply the status register. This register is set out like any other register or byte in memory, with eight bits (fingers). Each bit represents a flag for a different purpose:

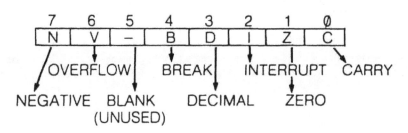

A list of which instructions set which flags can be seen in the table in Appendix 1.

1. The carry (C) flag, as we have already seen, is set or cleared to indicate a 'carry' or 'borrow' from the eighth bit of the byte into the 'ninth' bit. Since there is no ninth bit, it goes into the carry to be included in future calculations or ignored. The carry can be set or cleared using SEC and CLC respectively. A program can test for carry set or cleared using BCS or BCC respectively.

2. The zero (Z) flag, as we have already seen is set or cleared depending on the result of some operations, comparisons or transfers of data (Load or Store). A program can test for zero set or cleared by using BEQ or BNE respectively.

3. Setting the break (B) flag, using the BRK command causes what is known as an interrupt. More will be said about

interrupts in Chapter 11. Using a BRK will cause your machine language program to stop and the computer to jump indirect on the contents of $FFFE and $FFFF. These ROM addresses hold the address of a break routine which will return you to BASIC. Using the BRK command is a very effective way of debugging a program.

By inserting this command into your program at specific points, you will be able to trace (by whether the program stops or hangs) how far a program is getting before it does the wrong thing. The BRK command gives you the chance to stop a program and test the variables in memory to see if they hold the values you would expect at this point in the program. Use the BRK command with one of the programs from this book to practise using it as a debugging tool.

4. The interrupt (I) flag, may be set or cleared use SEI or CLI respectively. When set, the interrupt flag will disable certain types of interrupts from occurring (see Chapter 11).

5. The decimal (D) flag, may be set or cleared using the SED and CLD commands respectively. When the decimal flag is set the microproccesor goes into decimal or BCD mode. BCD stands for Binary Coded Decimal and is a method of representing decimal numbers within the computer's memory. In the BCD representation, hexadecimal digits Ø — 9 are read as their decimal equivalents and the digits A — F have no meaning. In other words:

BCD REPRESENTATION

Binary	Hex	Decimal value of BCD
ØØØØØØØØ	ØØ	Ø
ØØØØØØØ1	Ø1	1
ØØØØØØ1Ø	Ø2	2
ØØØØØØ11	Ø3	3
ØØØØØ1ØØ	Ø4	4
ØØØØØ1Ø1	Ø5	5
ØØØØØ11Ø	Ø6	6
ØØØØØ111	Ø7	7
ØØØØ1ØØØ	Ø8	8
ØØØØ1ØØ1	Ø9	9
ØØØ1ØØØØ	1Ø	1Ø
ØØØ1ØØØ1	11	11
ØØ1ØØØ1Ø	22	22
Ø1ØØØØ11	43	43
1ØØ11ØØØ	98	98

This shows that there are six possible codes between the values of 9 and 1Ø which are wasted.

In decimal mode the microprocessor automatically adds and subtracts BCD numbers, e.g.

Decimal Flag = Ø	Decimal Flag = 1
17	17
+26	+26
——	——
3D	43

The problems with decimal mode are that it is wasteful of memory and is very slow to use mathematically (apart from adds and subtracts). On the whole it is easier to use hex and convert for output, and so decimal mode is rarely used. Try converting some of the programs in this book to decimal mode and compare their output to normal calculations.

6. The negative flag. So far we have said that the only numbers that could be held within a single byte were those between Ø and 255. We have talked about dealing with numbers greater than 255 by using two bytes, but we have not mentioned anything about numbers less than zero. We have used them without realising it in Chapter 6. We have seen from our use of numbers Ø to 255 to represent anything from numbers to addresses, from characters to BCD numbers, that the microprocessor will behave the same no matter how we use these numbers. The memory might be a character an address or an instruction, but if we add one to it the microprocessor will not care what it is we are representing. It will just do it blindly.

In Chapter 6 we took our number between Ø and 255 and chose to use it as the value of a relative branch; we chose $ØØ to $7F as a forward (positive) and $8Ø to $FF as a backward (negative) branch. This numbering system is purely arbitrary but, as it turns out, it is mathematically sound to use it to represent positive and negative numbers. The system we use is called Two's Complement Arithmetic. We can use the tables in Appendix 3 to convert between normal numbers and Two's Complemnt numbers, looking for the number in decimal in the centre and finding the correct two's complement hex value on the outside. Mathematically, we take the complement of the binary number (all 1's become Ø's and all Ø's become 1's) and then add 1, e.g.,

COMPLEMENT

$3 = Ø Ø Ø Ø Ø Ø 1 1 \rightarrow$ | 1 | 1 | 1 | 1 | 1 | 1 | Ø | Ø |

$+1$

$= $ | 1 | 1 | 1 | 1 | 1 | 1 | Ø | 1 | $= FD = -3$

Using this representation, you will see that any byte whose value is greater than 127 (with its high bit, bit 7 turned on) represents a negative number, and any value less that 128 (high bit turned off) represents a positive number.

```
1 X X X X X X X  -  NEGATIVE
Ø X X X X X X X  -  POSITIVE
```

The negative flag in the status register is automatically set (like the zero flag) if any number used as the result of an operation, a comparison or transfer, is negative. Since the microprocessor cannot tell if the value it is dealing with represents a number, character or anything else, it always sets the negative flag, if the high bit of the byte being used is set. In other words, the negative flag is always a copy of bit 7 (high bit) of the result of an operation.

Since the high bit of a byte is a sign bit (representing the sign of the number) we are left with only seven bits to store the actual number. With seven bits you can represent any number between Ø and 127 but, since Ø = −Ø on the negative side we add one. So two's complement numbers can represent any number from −128 to +127 using one byte.

Let's try some mathematics using our new numbering system.

Two's Complement Binary   Decimal value

Positive + Positive (no different no normal)

```
  00000111                + 7
+ 00001001                ++ 9
  ─────────               ─────
  00010000                 16   C = Ø V = Ø N = Ø
```

Positive + Negative (negative result)

```
  00000111                + 7
+ 11110100                + −12
  ─────────               ─────
  11111011                 − 5   C = Ø V = Ø N = 1
```

Positive + Negative (positive result)

```
   00000111               + 7
+  11111101               + − 3
   ─────────              ─────
(1)00000100               + 4   C = 1 V = Ø N = Ø
```

Positive + Positive (answer greater than 127)

```
  01110011                115
+ 00110001                + 49
  ─────────               ─────
  10100100                −92   C = Ø V = 1 N = 1
```

NOTE: this answer is **wrong!**

84

Two's complement numbering system seems to handle positive and negative numbers well, except in our last example. We said previously that two's complement could only hold numbers from −128 to +127. The answer to our question should have been 164. As in Chapter 3, to hold a number greater than 255 we need two bytes, here also we must use two bytes. In normal binary a carry from bit 7 (high bit) into the high byte was done through the carry. In two's complement we have seen seven bits and a sign bit so the high bit is bit 6. The microprocessor, not knowing we are using two's complement arithmetic, has as usual 'carried' bit 6 into bit 7. To enable us to correct this, it has set the overflow flag to tell us this has happened.

7. The overflow flag. This flag is set by a carry from bit 6 into bit 7.

```
        7 6 5 4 3 2 1 0
e.g. [0|1|1|1|1|1|1|1] + [0|0|0|0|0|0|0|1] = [1|0|0|0|0|0|0|0]
         127          +         1          =         128
```

The major use of the overflow flag is in signalling the accidental change of sign caused by an 'overflow' using two's complement arithmetic. To correct for this accidental change of signs, the sign bit (bit 7) must be be complemented (inverted) and a one carried on to the high bit if necessary.

This would make our previously wrong result of −92 (10100100) become 1 x 128 (high byte) + 36 (00100100). 128 + 36 = 164 which is the correct answer.

A program can test for the negative flag being set or cleared using BMI (Branch on Minus) or BPL (Branch on Plus) respectively.

A program can test for the overflow flag being set or cleared using BVS (Branch on Overflow Set) or BVC (Branch on Overflow Clear) respectively. The overflow flag can be cleared using the CLV command.

Chapter 9   SUMMARY

1. The microprocessor contains a special purpose register, the processor status code register.

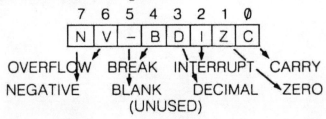

2. CARRY - SEC, CLC
          BCS, BCC

3. ZERO - BEQ, BNE
    Set if a result or transfer = $\emptyset$.

4. BRK is an instruction which sets the break flag and halts
the microprocessor (useful for debugging purposes).

5. INTERRUPT - SEI, CLI
    See Chapters 11, 12.

6. DECIMAL - SED, CLD
Sets decimal mode. Addition and subtraction are done using BCD
(Binary Coded Decimal).

7. Two's Complement numbering represents numbers from -128 to
+127.
      negative X = (complement (X)) + 1

8. NEGATIVE - flag set if bit 7 of result is turned on (=1)
          BMI, BPL

9. OVERFLOW - set on two's complement carry
          CLV
          BVS, BVC

Chapter 10
Logical Operators and Bit Manipulators

Changing bits within memory

In this Chapter we will be looking at a group of instructions unlike any we have looked at previously, yet they are absolutely fundamental to the workings of a computer. They are the 'logical' or 'Boolean' operations. They are the commands AND (Logical AND), ORA (Logical OR), and EOR (Logical Exclusive OR).

These functions can be built up using fairly simple circuitry, and almost all functions of the computer are built up by series of these circuits. The logical operations of these circuits are available to us through these instructions and it is this, and not the hardware, with which we will concern ourselves in this chapter.

We know that bytes of memory and the registers are made up of groups of eight bits:

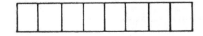

To explain the functions of these instructions, we look at their operation on one bit and then assume that this operation is done on all eight bits at once. A logical operator is like a mathematical function in that it takes two pieces of data and outputs the result as a single piece of data, e.g.,

$$4 + 5 = 9$$

In this case however the data coming in is going to be single bit values, either 1's or ∅'s. To define a logical function we draw up a truth table showing all possible inputs and the associated outputs.

INPUT 1 / INPUT 2	∅	1
∅	OUTPUT FOR ∅, ∅	OUTPUT FOR ∅, 1
1	OUTPUT FOR 1, ∅	OUTPUT FOR 1, 1

The logical AND

The first instruction we will deal with is the AND instruction. This performs a logical AND with the accumulator and the specified memory, leaving the result in A. The result of a logical AND is 1 if input one is a 1 and input two is a 1. The truth table for this function looks like:

AND

MEMORY / ACCUMULATOR	∅	1
∅	∅	∅
1	∅	1

When extended to an eight bit byte this means that:

```
        ∅ 1 1 ∅ 1 ∅ 1 1
AND     1 ∅ 1 1 1 ∅ 1 ∅
=       ∅ ∅ 1 ∅ 1 ∅ 1 ∅
```

The zero flag is set if the result = ∅, i.e. if there are no coincident ones in the bits of the two bytes used.

The AND instruction is useful in creating a 'mask' to turn off certain bits within a byte. Suppose, within a byte of any value, we wish to turn off the 3rd, 5th and 6th bits. We would create a 'mask' with only the 3rd, 5th and 6th bits turned off and AND this with the byte in question.

```
          7 6 5 4 3 2 1 0
Mask = | 1 | 0 | 0 | 1 | 0 | 1 | 1 | 1 |   = $97
```

AND #$97

would turn off the 3rd, 5th and 6th bits of whatever was in the accumulator.

The logical OR

The second instruction we will look at is the ORA instruction. This does a logical OR of the accumulator with the specified memory leaving the result in the accumulator. The OR function outputs a 1 if input one is a 1 or input two is a 1. The truth table for this function looks like:

OR	MEMORY	0	1
ACCUMULATOR			
0		0	1
1		1	1

When extended to an eight bit byte this means that:

```
      | 0 | 1 | 0 | 1 | 0 | 0 | 1 | 0 |
ORA   | 0 | 0 | 1 | 1 | 1 | 0 | 1 | 0 |
  =   | 0 | 1 | 1 | 1 | 1 | 0 | 1 | 0 |
```

The zero flag is set if both bytes are equal to zero and hence the result is zero.

The ORA instruction is useful for turning on certain bits within a byte using the masking technique.

Supposing we want to turn on the 2nd, 3rd and 7th bits within a byte. We would use a mask with only the 2nd, 3rd and 7th bits turned on.

```
          7 6 5 4 3 2 1 0
Mask  =  | 1 | 0 | 0 | 0 | 1 | 1 | 0 | 0 |  = $8C
ORA  #$8C
```

would turn on the 2nd, 3rd and 7th bits of whatever was in the accumulator.

89

The logical Exclusive OR

The last of the logical operations is the EOR. This performs a logical exclusive OR of the accumulator and memory leaving the result in A. The exclusive OR function outputs a 1 if input one is a 1 or input two is a 1 but not if both are 1. The truth table for this function looks like:

EOR	MEMORY	0	1
ACCUMULATOR			
0		0	1
1		1	0

When extended to an eight bit byte the exclusive OR produces:

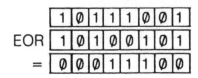

```
      1 0 1 1 1 0 0 1
EOR   1 0 1 0 0 1 0 1
 =    0 0 0 1 1 1 0 0
```

The exclusive OR is used to complement (invert) bits within a byte using masking.

To invert the 1st, 2nd and 4th bits of a byte we would use a mask with those bits turned on

```
       7 6 5 4 3 2 1 0
Mask = 0 0 0 1 0 1 1 0  = $16
EOR #$16
```

would invert those bits of the accumulator.

Type the following program into ALPA to test these instructions:

```
NEW
APPEND

1                    ORG $0600
2                    PLA
3                    LDA #$CA
```

```
4                    AND #$9F
5                    STA $Ø3FD
6                    LDA #$A2
7                    ORA #$84
8                    EOR $Ø3FD
9                    STA $Ø3FD
1Ø                   RTS
```

WATCH
(What address)? Ø3FD

Program summary


```
Line 3   LDA #$CA   A = $CA    11ØØ1Ø1Ø
Line 4   AND #$9F   A = $8A    1ØØØ1Ø1Ø
Line 5   STA $Ø3FD  A = $Ø3FD  1ØØØ1Ø1Ø
Line 6   LDA #$A2   A = $A2    1Ø1ØØØ1Ø
Line 7   ORA #$84   A = $A6    1Ø1ØØ11Ø
Line 8   EOR $Ø3FD  A = $2C    ØØ1Ø11ØØ
```


ASM and RUN this program

and verify the results with those we have reached.

The bit instruction

There is a useful instruction in the 65Ø2 instruction set which
performs an interesting set of tests and comparisions. We
discussed in Chapter 6 how a CMP command did a subtraction
setting the status flags but not storing the result. Similarly
BIT (compare memory bits with the accumulator) performs a
logical AND of A with memory setting only the Z flag as a
result. The bit instruction also copies bit 7 into the
negative flag and bit 6 into the overflow flag.

Rotating bits within a byte

We will now discuss four other bit manipulation instructions
and some of their consequences. The first instruction we will
look at is ASL (Arithmetic Shift Left). This instruction
shifts all the bits in the specified byte left by one bit,
introducing a zero at the low end and moving the high bit into
the carry flag.

91

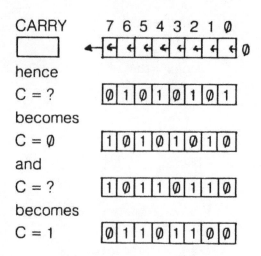

CARRY   7 6 5 4 3 2 1 0

hence
C = ? |0|1|0|1|0|1|0|1|

becomes
C = 0 |1|0|1|0|1|0|1|0|

and
C = ? |1|0|1|1|0|1|1|0|

becomes
C = 1 |0|1|1|0|1|1|0|0|

Back in Chapter 3 when we explained hex and binary we mentioned that each bit had a value of 2 to the power of position -1

i.e. |128|64|32|16|8|4|2|1|

You will notice that the value of each box is two times the value of the box to the right of it, hence:

    00000001 x 2 = 00000010 and
    00001000 x 2 = 00010000

and furthermore

    00111001 x 2 = 01110010

The operation required to multiply any byte by two is the operation performed by the ASL instruction.

    To use our examples from before:

C = ?   01010101 ($55) x 2 -> C = 0   10101010 ($AA)

C = ?   10110110 ($B6) x 2 -> C = 1   01101100 ($6C+CARRY)

Type in the following program:

```
NEW
APPEND


1                       ORG $Ø6ØØ
2                       PLA
3                       LDA #$ØA
4                       ASL
5                       STA $Ø3FD
6                       RTS

WATCH
(What address )? Ø3FD

ASM and RUN
```

Line 4 uses the 'accumulator' addressing mode. It uses the contents of the accumulator as data and returns the data there.

NOTE: this is different to implied addressing because ASL may be used on data from memory.

We can use this instruction to multiply a number by any power of 2 (1,2,4,8...). To use the previous program to multiply by eight instead of two, insert the following two lines:

```
1                       ORG $Ø6ØØ
2                       PLA
3                       LDA #$ØA
4                       ASL
5                       ASL
6                       ASL
7                       STA $Ø3FD
8                       RTS
```

ASM and RUN the program with these alterations:

$ØA x 8 = $5Ø

Rotation with carry

As with our addition routines, we may find we want to multiply numbers greater than 255 (two or more byte numbers). To do

93

this there is a shift command which uses the carry on the input end of the shift as well as the output end:

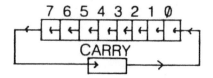

The instruction to do this is ROL (Rotate One bit Left). To do a two byte multiply by four, type in the following lines:

```
1           ORG $0600
2           PLA
3           LDA #$17
4           STA $03FE
5           LDA #$0A
6           ASL
7           ROL $03FE
8           ASL
9           ROL $03FE
10          STA $03FD
11          RTS
```

    LIST

NOTE:
1. To avoid swapping registers we have used ROL absolute which stores its result back in memory.

2. We have rotated both bytes once and then rotated both again. Rotating the low byte twice and then the high byte twice would not work, because the high bit from the low byte would be lost when the carry was used in the second ASL.

    ASM
    WATCH
    (What Address)? 03FE
    RUN

Put together the high and low bytes of the answer and check that it equals four times the original number.

Rotating to the right

LSR and ROR are the equivalent instructions to ASL and ROR, except that they shift the bits in the opposite direction.

94

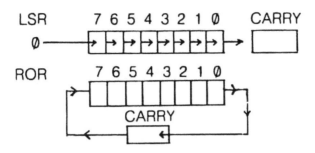

Just as their opposites can be thought of as multiplication by two, so these can be thought of as division by two, and can be similarly extended to multi-byte arithmetic. After division the number left in the byte is the integer part of the result and the bits that have been shifted out represent the remainder, e.g.,

$$\$1D \div \$08 \;=\; 3 \qquad \text{remainder } 5$$

	00011101	= 29	remainder
LSR	÷ 2		
	00001110	= 14	→ 1 = 1
LSR	÷ 4		
	00000111	= 7	→ 01 = 1
LSR	÷ 8		
	00000011	= 3	→ 101 = 5

NOTE: Just because the shift and rotate instructions can be used for arithmetic do not forget their use for shifting bits, e.g., shifting into carry for testing.

Clever multiplication

We have said that by shifting bits we can multiply by any power of 2 (1,2,4,8,..., 128). These are the same values that represent each bit within a byte. We have shown in Chapter 3 that by adding these values we can produce any number between 0 and 255.

If we then multiply by each of these values and add the results, this process is then equivalent to multiplying by any value from 0 to 255, e.g.,

$$
\begin{aligned}
\$16 \times \$59 \;=\;\; & 00010110 \times \$59 \\
+\; & 00010000 \times \$59 \\
+\; & 00000100 \times \$59 \\
+\; & 00000010 \times \$59 \\[6pt]
=\; & 16 \times \$59 + 4 \times \$59 + 2 \times \$59
\end{aligned}
$$

95

which we know how to work out from our previous multiplication.

This is the algorithm we will use in our generalised multiplication routine. We will rotate (multiply by two) one number, and add it to total, for each bit turned on in the other byte, e.g.,

$10110 \times \$59$
rotate $59   1 0 1 1 [0]
rotate $59   add to total   1 0 1 [1] 0
rotate $59   add to total   1 0 [1] 1 0
rotate $59   1 [0] 1 1 0
rotate $59   add to total   [1] 0 1 1 0

For simplicity's sake our generalised multiplication routine will only handle results less than 255.

To multiply $1B by $09 type:

NEW
APPEND

```
1                    ORG $0600
2                    PLA
3                    LDA #$1B
4                    STA $03FD
5                    LDA #$09
6                    STA $03FE
7                    LDA #$00
8                    ROR $03FE
9   LOOP             ROL $03FE
10                   LSR $03FD
11                   BCC &LOOP1
12                   CLC
13                   ADC $03FE
14  LOOP1            BNE &LOOP
15                   STA $03FF
16                   RTS
```

Program summary

Lines 1 – 8   Initialise values to be multiplied and set the total to 0. The ROR followed by the ROL has no effect the first time through but only the ROL is within the loop.

Line 9   Except for the first time through this   multiplies
one of the numbers (2) by each time round the loop.

Lines 1∅-11   Rotates the other number (1) bit by bit   into   the
carry, and then tests the carry to see if the other   number   (2)
should be added this time around the   loop.   If   the   carry   is
clear, the possibility that the   number   (1)   has   been   shifted
completely through (=∅ - multiplication is completed) is   tested
line 12∅

Lines 12-13   Add to the total (in A) the number   (2)   which   is
being multiplied by two each time around the loop.

Line   14   If the branch on line   9∅   was   taken,   this   will
test for the end of   multiplication   (number   (1)   =   ∅   shifted
completely through).   If the branch on line 9∅   was   not   taken,
this branch on not equal will always   be   true   because   we   are
adding a number (2) greater than zero to a total which will   not
be greater than 255.

Lines 15-16   end

NOTE: this multiplication routine is much more   efficient   than
the one given in Chapter 7.   By that method we   would   have   had
to loop at least nine times, whereas in   this,   had   we   swapped
and used 9 as number (1) and $1B as number (2),   we   would   have
only looped four times (number   of   bits   needed   to   make   9   -
6/∅1).

        WATCH
        (What address)? ∅3FE
        ASM
        RUN

and verify the results.

Now change the numbers in lines 3 and 5 with DELETE and   INSERT,
used to perform a different calculation (make   sure   the   answer
is >256), e.g.,

        3   LDA #$∅6
        5   LDA #$25

        ASM and RUN

with these values and again verify the results for yourself.

Chapter 10 SUMMARY

1. AND

   most often used to mask **off** bits.

2. ORA

   most often used to mask **on** bits.

3. EOR (exclusive or)

   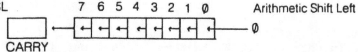 most often used to mask **invert** bits.

4. BIT   performs AND without storing the result.

   Z is set or cleared
   N becomes bit 7
   V becomes bit 6

5. ASL   Arithmetic Shift Left

   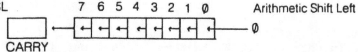

   CARRY

   most often used to multiply by 2.

6. ROL   Rotate One Bit Left

   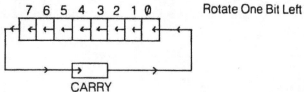

   CARRY

7. LSR   Logical Shift Right

   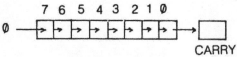

   CARRY

8. ROR   Rotate One Bit Right

   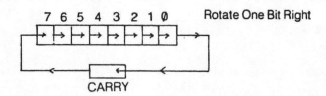

   CARRY

Chapter 11
Details of Program Counter

The program counter

We have talked a lot about the different operations that the microprocessor can perform, but we have said very little about how it goes about those tasks. This is perfectly alright, because in most cases we don't need to know. In one case, however, knowing how the microprocessor is operating leads us to a whole new category of commands and a powerful area of the microprocessor's capabilities.

The microprocessor contains a special purpose two byte register called the program counter (PC), whose sole job it is to keep track of where the next instruction is coming from in memory. In other words the program counter contains the address of the next byte to be loaded into the microprocessor and used as an instruction.

If we again turn to our post office boxes, each holding either an instruction (opcode) or the data/address it operates on (operand), this is what our program looks like:

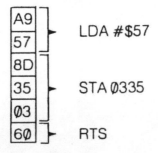

To 'run' our post office box program, we would go through each box in turn and act on the data in the box. Now imagine there was a large clock type counter showing a box address which we looked at to know which box to find. Normally this counter would go up one by one, taking the next byte in order. However, if it wanted us to move to a new area of the boxes, it would just flash up the address of the next instruction it wanted us to find. This is exactly how the JMP command operates.

Storing into the program counter

The instruction JMP $address only loads the two byte address into the program counter, the next instruction is then loaded from memory at that address, and a JMP has been executed.

NOTE: the branch instructions add or subtract from the program counter in a similar way, thereby creating a 'relative' jump. However branch instructions may only be in the range +129 to -126.

The program counter and subroutines

If it were possible to store the program counter just before doing a JMP and changing it to a new address, we would later be able to return to the same place in memory by reloading that stored piece of memory back into the program counter. In other words, if we had noticed that the post office box counter was about to change, and we noted down the address it showed (our current address) before it changed, we would at some future stage place that back on the program counter and return to where we had left off.

This of course, is a subroutine structure, e.g.,

```
10 PRINT "HELLO THERE"
20 GOSUB 100
30 PRINT "I'M FINE"
40 END
100 PRINT "HOW ARE YOU TODAY ?"
110 RETURN
```

would print:

```
HELLO THERE
HOW ARE YOU TODAY ?
I'M FINE
```

We said at the beginning of the book that a machine language program can be thought of as a subroutine called from BASIC using the USR command.

You can also create subroutines from within a machine language program. They are called using the JSR (Jump to SubRoutine) command. As when called from BASIC, to return from a machine language subroutine you use the RTS (ReTurn from Subroutine) command.

Type in the following program:

```
1                          ORG $Ø6ØØ
2    BACK                  EQU $Ø2C8
3                          PLA
4    LOOP                  INC BACK
5                          JSR WAIT
6                          JMP LOOP
7    WAIT                  LDX #$FF
8    DELAY                 DEX
9                          BNE &DELAY
1Ø                         RTS


ASM
RUN
```

This program will increment the border color register ($Ø2C8) and the border will become a mass of different colored horizontal bars. The vertical height of the color bars depends on the delay loop in the routine. The bigger the delay the greater the bars height. Remember that these programs go extremely fast. This program uses an infinite loop so to get back to ASM it will be nessary to press RESET and GOTO 12.

It is good programming style to use subroutines for two major reasons. First, it is easy to locate and fix errors within subroutines. Secondly, by using subroutines it is possible to build up a 'libary' of useful subroutines for regular use.

We have said that the return address of the routine is stored away but we have not said anything about how it is stored. We want some sort of filing system to store this address which will give us a number of necessary features.

The stack control structure

Firstly it must be flexible and easy to use. Secondly, we would like to be able to provide for the possibility that a subroutine will be called from within a subroutine (called from within a subroutine, called from......). In this case we have to use a system that will not only remember a return address for each of the subroutines called, but will also have to remember which is the correct return address for each subroutine. The system which we use to store the addresses on a data structure is called a 'stack'. A stack is a LIFO structure (Last In First Out). When an RTS is reached, we want the last address put on the stack to be used as a return address for the subroutine.

101

Imagine the stack to be one of those spikes that people sometimes keep messages on.

Every time you see a JSR instruction, you copied down the return address onto a piece of paper from the post office box counter. As soon as you had done this, you spiked the piece of paper on the stack. If you came across another piece of paper you merely repeated the process. Now when you come across an RTS, the only piece of paper you can take of the spike (stack) is the top one. The others are all blocked by those on top of them. This top piece of paper will always contain the correct address for the subroutine that you are returning from (the one most recently called).

Subroutines and the stack

The JSR and RTS commands do this automatically using the system stack. The stack sits in memory from $1\emptyset\emptyset$ to $1FF (Page 1) and grows downwards. Imagine the spike turned upside down. This makes no difference to its operation. The top of the stack (actually the bottom) is marked by a special purpose register within the microprocessor called the Stack Pointer (S). When a JSR is performed the two byte program counter is placed on the stack and the stack pointer (SP) is decremented by two (a two byte address is placed on the stack).

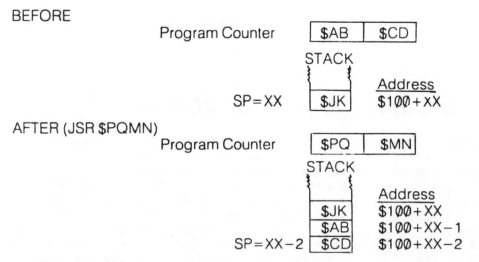

BEFORE

AFTER (JSR $PQMN)

An RTS takes the top two bytes off the stack and returns them to the program counter. The stack pointer is incremented by two.

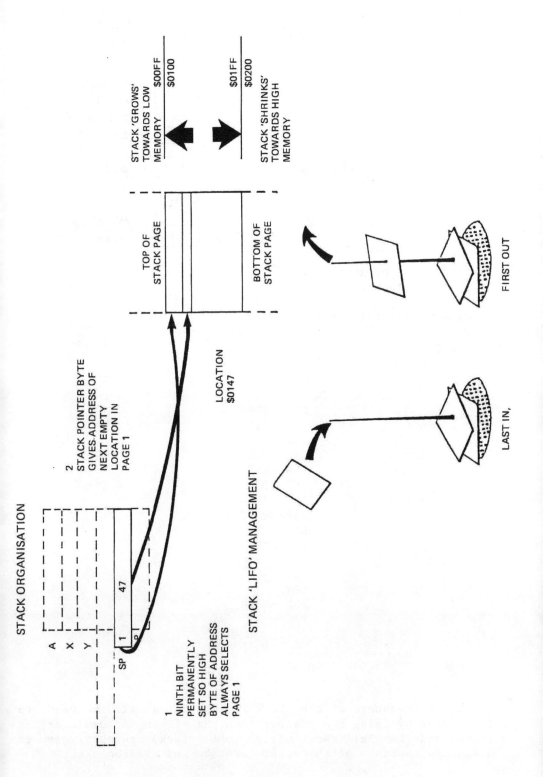

STACK ORGANISATION

A
X
Y
SP | 1 | 47 | P |

1
NINTH BIT
PERMANENTLY
SET SO HIGH
BYTE OF ADDRESS
ALWAYS SELECTS
PAGE 1

2
STACK POINTER BYTE
GIVES ADDRESS OF
NEXT EMPTY
LOCATION IN
PAGE 1

LOCATION
$0147

STACK 'LIFO' MANAGEMENT

LAST IN,

FIRST OUT

TOP OF
STACK PAGE

BOTTOM OF
STACK PAGE

STACK 'GROWS'
TOWARDS LOW
MEMORY $00FF
                $0100

STACK 'SHRINKS'
TOWARDS HIGH $01FF
MEMORY $0200

BEFORE

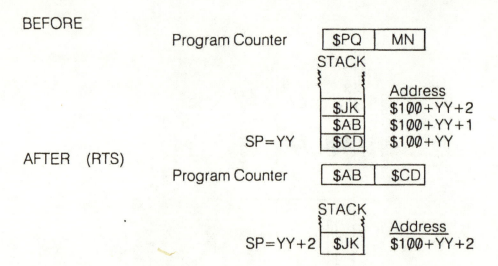

The following program is an example of calling a subroutine from within a subroutine. This is the previous program with an extra delay being called in WAIT named MWAIT. As a result the vertical bars will get higher.

```
        NEW
        APPEND


1                       ORG $0600
2       BACK            EQU $02C8
3                       PLA
4       LOOP            INC BACK
5                       JSR WAIT
6                       JMP LOOP
7       WAIT            LDX #$FF
8       DELAY           JSR MWAIT
9                       DEX
10                      BNE &DELAY
11                      RTS
12      MWAIT           LDY #$10
13      MORE            DEY
14                      BNE &MORE
15                      RTS
```

ASM and RUN the program.

One major advantage of the stack is that it can also be used to store data by using the instructions PHA (Push Accumulator on stack) and PLA (Pull Accumulator off stack) respectively to place the contents of the accumulator on and off the stack.

WARNING: make sure you put things on and off the stack in the correct order or your machine will not speak to you until you have reset it!

If you use an RTS while there is extra data on top of the stack, the RTS will return an address made up of the two top bytes of the stack, whatever they are.

Let's use these instructions to test the operation of the stack. Type:

```
NEW
WATCH (address?  Ø3FD)


1                       ORG $Ø6ØØ
2    BACK               EQU $Ø2C8
3                       PLA
4                       JSR SAVE
5                       INC BACK (border)
6                       RTS
7    SAVE               PLA
8                       TAX
9                       PLA
1Ø                      STX $Ø3FD
11                     ·STA $Ø3FE
12                      PHA
13                      TXA
14                      PHA
15                      RTS
```

Program summary

Lines 1- 3   Set the ORG, the value of background register and balance the stack

Line 4   JSR – return address (address of next instruction is placed on stack). Actually it points to the byte before the next instruction because the PC is incremented each time before a byte is 'fetched' from memory.

Line 5   Increments screen border colour (see Appendix 6) just to show that the program has returned satisfactorily.

Line 6   end.

Lines 7- 9   Take the top two bytes of the stack

Lines 1∅-11   Store them low byte - high byte at $3FD, $3FE.

Lines 12-14   Return bytes to stack in correct order

Line 15   End of subroutine.

ASM and RUN this program. Change WATCH to test address $∅3FE, and RUN again. Put the results together and compare them with the expected address.

The two instructions TSX (Transfer SP into X) and TXS (Transfer X into SP) are available to do direct manipualations on the SP. Write a progam with a subroutine within a subroutine, both of which save the SP in memory via X to see the change in SP when a subroutine is called and when an RTS is executed.

The stack and interrupts

We mentioned in Chapter 9 the BRK command and its use in debugging programs by halting them and allowing you to examine variables in 'mid-flight'. What the BRK command actually does is something like the operation of a JSR. The BRK command performs a JSR indirect to $FFFE, $FFFF. In other words the contents of these bytes are placed in the PC and the program continues there (at a ROM break handling routine). The BRK command also pushes the value of the processor status code (P) onto the stack.

This can be done outside the BRK command using the PHP (Push Processor Status byte) instruction. This all leads up to a fairly major area of machine language programming on the ATARI 13∅XE - Interrupts. However we will not cover these as they are too advanced for this book but we will attempt to tell you how, where and why they work.

In general an interrupt is sent to the microprocessor by the computer's hardware to alert it to something going on in the outside world which requires its attention, e.g, a key being pressed, a real time clock, or graphics alerts (see Chapter 12 and Appendix 6 respectively).

These interrupts are hardware signals and their effect is to stop the microprocessor, no matter what it's doing, and jump to an interrupt service routine (via vectors at $FFFE and $FFFF).

In a similar way to the BRK command an interrupt stores the PC on the stack (with the address of the instruction it was in the

106

middle of doing – not the next instruction). It then stores the status register (P) on the stack and does an indirect jump on the contents of $FFFE, $FFFF which take it to a ROM interrupt routine.

You can control the interrupt service routines to handle interrupts from clock timers or other sources in your own way, to do things such as move objects at a constant predetermined speed and increment time of day clocks as well as many other uses. Some of the methods for doing this are described in the next chapter.

Press RESET to return the screen to normal and type GOTO 12.

Chapter 11 SUMMARY

1. Program counter (PC) points to the next byte in memory minus one to be used as an instruction.

2. JMP loads an address into the PC.

3. Branches add or subtract from the PC.

4. JSR stores the PC on stack and loads the new address into the PC (subroutine).

5. RTS takes the top two bytes off the stack and loads them into PC (return address).

6. The stack can only have things put on at one end. They can only be taken off from the same end and in the same order they were put on.

7. The Stack Pointer keeps track of the top of the stack.

        RTS = > SP = SP + 2
        JSR = > SP = SP - 2

8. PHA, PLA store and retrieve the accumulator from the stack. Be sure to take things off the stack in the same order they went on.

9. TXS, TSX transfer data betweem the stack register (S) and the X register.

10. BRK   PC   - > Stack (2 bytes)
        Status byte   - > Stack
        Contents of
        (FFFE, FFFF)   - > PC

11. PHP, PLP push and pull a processor status word onto the stack.

12. Interrupts come from chips external to the microprocessor.

```
          PC               - > Stack (2 bytes)
   Status byte             - > Stack
   (FFFE, FFFF)            PC
```

These are processed by the ROM handling routines.

Chapter 12
Dealing with the Operating System

The Kernal

This chapter will tell you something about dealing with the operating system of the Atari 13ØXE. It sits in memory from $E4ØØ to $FFFF and deals with the hardware side of the computer (the other ROM deals with BASIC). The kernal ROM actually starts at $EØØØ but the first one kilobyte is taken up by the character set. There are routines in the kernal for opening and closing files, printing characters to the screen, getting characters from the keyboard, moving the cursor around the screen, loading and saving files and other such mundane but necessary tasks.

In this chapter we will give examples of how to use a few of these routines (the Appendices will give clues to more but the rest is up to you). Armed with these methods and the information given in the Appendices (and any other literature you have handy), you will be able to create programs that can easily and efficiently communicate with the outside world.

One of the major uses of the kernal is in dealing with interrupts. Interrupts can be caused by peripherals, the sound chip, the clock and many other places. The clock sends out an interrupt every 1/5Ø a second (1/6Ø in the U.S.A.). This interrupt is used by the kernal to update the time of day clock and to check the keyboard for a keypress.

We said in the previous chapter that an interrupt, as well as putting a return address and the status byte on the stack, performed an indirect JMP on the contents of memory locations $FFFE and $FFFF. We said that this was directed to the operating system's interrupt handling routine in ROM. This ROM routine does its work and then gives the programmer access to the interrupt process by doing a jump through interrupt vectors placed in RAM at locations $Ø222, $Ø223 (low byte — high byte format). Since these vectors are placed in RAM they can be changed to point to our program.

Our interrupt routine must do one of two things. It must either return via the operating system when it is finished (via the address that was in the interrupt vector before we changed it) or we must 'clean' up the system and return properly from an interrupt. In practice it is generally easier to take the first choice. If we do it on our own the program must finish by:

1. Taking the registers off the stack. When the ROM interrupt routine is called it saves all the registers on the stack. These must be returned to the registers in the same order.

2. We must re-enable interrupts. The ROM routine as well as doing a SEI which sets the interrupt flag in the status register turns off the interrupts from their source.

3. Do an RTI (ReTurn from Interrupt).

NOTE: SEI (Set Interrupt Flag) will make the microprocessor ignore any interrupts but will not stop any devices from issuing interrupts. This instruction is executed at the beginning of the interrupt routine by the 6502 automatically to make sure that the interrupt is not interrupted by another interrupt. Any time-critical code should have this at the start of it to stop interrupts from interfering with it's timing.

CLI (Clear Interrupt Flag)

Re-enables interrupts to the 6502 processor. This instruction is used at the end of some interrupt routines, or if the interrupt is non time-critical.

RTI (Return From Interrupt)

Somewhat like the RTS, this instruction removes those things placed on the stack by the interrupt (status byte, program counter), thereby returning to where the program left off (with status byte undisturbed). This, by restoring the status byte will clear the interrupt flag (it could not have been set when the interrupt was received!)

Our sample interrupt program which follows is in two parts. The first part sets up the vertical blank interrupt vector at

110

$\emptyset222$, $\emptyset223$; it is called once when the program is RUN and
then returns. The SEI instruction disables interrupts while
the interrupt vector is being changed. Otherwise an interrupt
could occur while the routine had only half changed the vector
and the machine would crash. After the vector is changed,
interrupts are re-enabled and control is passed back to BASIC.

The second part which is pointed to by the altered interrupt
vectors, is called 5$\emptyset$ times a second (when an vertical blank
interrupt occurs). All this the routine does is invert the
first 255 characters on the screen every time a vertical
interrupt happens. So the top of the screen will flicker
between spaces and CHR$(255) very quickly.

```
NEW
APPEND
1                   ORG  $Ø6ØØ
2                   PLA
3                   SEI
4                   LDA  #$ØE
5                   STA  $Ø222
6                   LDA  #$Ø6
7                   STA  $Ø223
8                   CLI
9                   RTS
1Ø   WRITE          STA  ACCUM
11                  STX  XREG
12                  LDX  #$FF
13   LOOP           LDA  $9C4Ø,X
14                  EOR  #$FF
15                  STA  $9C4Ø,X
16                  DEX
17                  BNE  &LOOP
18                  LDX  XREG
19                  LDA  ACCUM
2Ø                  JMP  $C28A
21   ACCUM          DFB  $ØØ
22   XREG           DFB  $ØØ
```

Program summary

Line	2	Balance the system stack
Lines	3	Disable system interrupts
Lines	4- 7	Point at the new interrupt vector
Line	8	Re-enable the interrupts
Line	9	Return from the routine
Lines	1Ø-11	Save the accumulator and X register
Lines	12-17	Invert the first 255 characters on the screen

111

Lines 18–19	Restore accumulator and X register to their orginal value
Line 2Ø	Jump to the normal vertical blank interrupt routine
Line 21–22	Area to store accumulator and the X register

If you add your own interrupt routine to the machine and you want BASIC to continue functioning, then you must at the end of your routine jump to the normal interrupt routine. This is what the JMP $C28A does. Use the disassembler to study the operating system and BASIC

THE BEST OF BRITISH TO YOU!

Oh! There is one 65Ø2 instruction which has only been vaguely mentioned. That is NOP (No Operation) instruction. Although it does nothing it takes a certain amount of time to do (two machine cycles). It is used surprisingly often within a time delay loop, or to fill a patch within a program where you have decided to remove instructions (bad programming!). The value for the instruction NOP is $EA.

Chapter 12 SUMMARY

1.   The Kernal, which is in ROM, handles the computer's contact with the outside world.

2.   Kernal resides in memory from $E4ØØ to $FFFF.

3.   SEI – sets the interrupt flag to false and makes the 65Ø2 ignore any further interrupts.

4.   CLI – clears the interrupt flag, re-enables interrupts.

5.   RTI   –>   return from interrupt.
     STACK –>   Status byte
     STACK –>   PC (2 bytes)

6.   NOP   –>   no operation.

Appendix 1
6502 Instruction Codes

These tables should be a constant reference while writing machine language or assembly language programs. There is a list of every instruction with a description, avialable addressing modes, instruction format, number of bytes used, the hex code for the instruction and a list of the status flags changed as a result of the operation.

6502 MICROPROCESSOR INSTRUCTIONS IN ALPHABETICAL ORDER

ADC	Add Memory to Accumulator with Carry	JSR	Jump to New Location Saving Return Address
AND	"AND" Memory with Accumulator	LDA	Load Accumulator with Memory
ASL	Shift Left One Bit (Memory or Accumulator)	LDX	Load Index X with Memory
BCC	Branch on Carry Clear	LDY	Load Index Y with Memory
BCS	Branch on Carry Set	LSR	Shift Right one Bit (Memory or Accumulator)
BEQ	Branch on Result Zero		
BIT	Test Bits in Memory with Accumulator	NOP	No Operation
		ORA	"OR" Memory with Accumulator
BMI	Branch on Result Minus	PHA	Push Accumulator on Stack
BNE	Branch on Result not Zero	PHP	Push Processor Status on Stack
BPL	Branch on Result Plus	PLA	Pull Accumulator from Stack
BRK	Force Break	PLP	Pull Processor Status from Stack
BVC	Branch on Overflow Clear	ROL	Rotate One Bit Left (Memory or Accumulator)
BVS	Branch on Overflow Set		
CLC	Clear Carry Flag	ROR	Rotate One Bit Right (Memory or Accumulator)
CLD	Clear Decimal Mode		
CLI	Clear Interrupt Disable Bit	RTI	Return from Interrupt
CLV	Clear Overflow flag	RTS	Return from Subroutine
CMP	Compare Memory and Accumulator	SBC	Subtract Memory from Accumulator with Borrow
CPX	Compare Memory and Index X	SEC	Set Carry Flag
CPY	Compare Memory and Index Y	SED	Set Decimal Mode
DEC	Decrement Memory by One	SEI	Set Interrupt Disable Status
DEX	Decrement Index X by One	STA	Store Accumulator in Memory
DEY	Decrement Index Y by One	STX	Store Index X in Memory
EOR	"Exclusive-Or" Memory with Accumulator	STY	Store Index Y in Memory
		TAX	Transfer Accumulator to Index X
INC	Increment Memory by One	TAY	Transfer Accumulator to Index Y
INX	Increment Index X by One	TSX	Transfer Stack Pointer to Index X
INY	Increment Index Y by One	TXA	Transfer Index X to Accumulator
JMP	Jump to New Location	TXS	Transfer Index X to Stack Pointer
		TYA	Transfer Index Y to Accumulator

6502 INSTRUCTION CODES

Name Description	Addressing Mode	Assembly Language Form	No Bytes	HEX OP Code	Status Register
ADC Add memory to accumulator with carry	Immediate Zero Page Zero Page.X Absolute Absolute.X Absolute.Y (Indirect.X) (Indirect).Y	ADC #Oper ADC Oper ADC Oper.X ADC Oper ADC Oper.X ADC Oper.Y AND (Oper.X) ADC (Oper).Y	2 2 2 3 3 3 2 2	69 65 75 6D 7D 79 61 71	N V - B D I Z C • • • •
AND "AND" memory with accumulator	Immediate Zero Page Zero Page.X Absolute Absolute.X Absolute.Y (Indirect.X) (Indirect).Y	AND #Oper AND Oper AND Oper.X AND Oper AND Oper.X AND Oper.Y AND (Oper.X) AND (Oper.)Y	2 2 2 3 3 3 2 2	29 25 35 2D 3D 39 31 31	N V - B D I Z C • •
ASL Shift left one bit (Memory or Accumulator) C◄7 6 5 4 3 2 1 0◄0	Accumulator Zero Page Zero Page.X Absolute Absolute.X	ASL A ASL Oper ASL Oper.X ASL Oper ASL Oper.X	1 2 2 3 3	0A 06 16 0E 1E	N V - B D I Z C • • •
BCC Branch on carry clear	Relative	BCC Oper	2	90	N V - B D I Z C
BCS Branch on carry set	Relative	BCS Oper	2	B0	N V - B D I Z C
BEQ Branch on result zero	Relative	BEQ Oper	2	F0	N V - B D I Z C
BIT Test bits in memory with accumulator	Zero Page Absolute	BIT Oper BIT Oper	1 3	24 2C	N V - B D I Z C M M • 7 6
BMI Branch on result minus	Relative	BMI Oper	2	30	N V - B D I Z C
BNE Branch on result not zero	Relative	BNE Oper	2	D0	N V - B D I Z C
BPL Branch on result plus	Relative	BPL oper	2	10	N V - B D I Z C
BRK Force Break	Implied	BRK	1	00	N V - B D I Z C 1 1
BVC Branch on overflow clear	Relative	BVC Oper	2	50	N V - B D I Z C

Name Description	Addressing Mode	Assembly Language Form	No Bytes	HEX OP Code	Status Register
BVS Branch on overflow set	Relative	BVS Oper	2	70	N V - B D I Z C
CLC Clear carry flag	Implied	CLC	1	18	N V - B D I Z C 0
CLD Clear decimal mode	Implied	CLD	1	D8	N V - B D I Z C 0
CLI Clear interrupt flag	Implied	CLI	1	58	N V - B D I Z C 0
CLV Clear overflow flag	Implied	CLV	1	B8	N V - B D I Z C 0
CMP Compare memory and accumulator	Immediate Zero Page Zero Page.X Absolute Absolute.X Absolute.Y (Indirect.X) (Indirect).Y	CMP #Oper CMP Oper CMP Oper.X CMP Oper CMP Oper.X CMP Oper.Y CMP (Oper.X) CMP (Oper).Y	2 2 2 3 3 3 2 2	C9 C5 D5 CD DD D9 C1 D1	N V - B D I Z C • • •
CPX Compare memory and index X	Immediate Zero Page Absolute	CPX #Oper CPX Oper CPX Oper	2 2 3	E0 E4 EC	N V - B D I Z C • • •
CPY Compare memory and index Y	Immediate Zero Page Absolute	CPY #Oper CPY Oper CPY Oper	2 2 3	C0 C4 CC	N V - B D I Z C • • •
DEC Decrement memory by one	Zero Page Zero Page.X Absolute Absolute.X	DEC Oper DEC Oper.X DEC Oper DEC Oper.X	2 2 3 3	C6 D6 CE DE	N V - B D I Z C • •
DEX Decrement index X by one	Implied	DEX	1	DA	N V - B D I Z C • •
DEY Decrement index Y by one	Implied	DEY	1	88	N V - B D I Z C • •

Name Description	Addressing Mode	Assembly Language Form	No Bytes	HEX OP Code	Status Register
EOR "Exclusive Or" memory with accumulator	Immediate	EOR #Oper	2	49	N V - B D I Z C • •
	Zero Page	EOR Oper	2	45	
	Zero Page X	EOR Oper.X	2	55	
	Absolute	EOR Oper	3	4D	
	Absolute.X	EOR Oper.X	3	5D	
	Absolute.Y	EOR Oper.Y	3	59	
	(Indirect.X)	EOR (Oper.X)	2	41	
	(Indirect).Y	EOR (Oper).Y	2	51	
INC Increment memory by one	Zero Page	INC. Oper	2	E6	N V - B D I Z C • •
	Zero Page.X	INC Oper.X	2	F6	
	Absolute	INC Oper	3	EE	
	Absolute.X	INC Oper.X	3	FE	
INX Increment index X by one	Implied	INX	1	E8	N V - B D I Z C • •
INY Increment index Y by one	Implied	INY	1	C8	N V - B D I Z C • •
JMP Jump to new location	Absolute	JMP Oper	3	4C	N V - B D I Z C
	Indirect	JMP (Oper)	3	6C	
JSR Jump to new location saving return address	Absolute	JSR Oper	3	20	N V - B D I Z C
LDA Load accumulator with memory	Immediate	LDA #Oper	2	A9	N V - B D I Z C • •
	Zero Page	LDA Oper	2	A5	
	Zero Page.X	LDA Oper.X	2	B5	
	Absolute	LDA Oper	3	AD	
	Absolute.X	LDA Oper.X	3	BD	
	Absolute.Y	LDA Oper.Y	3	B9	
	(Indirect X)	LDA (Oper.X)	2	A1	
	(Indirect).Y	LDA (Oper).Y	2	B1	
LDX Load index X with memory	Immediate	LDX #Oper	2	A2	N V - B D I Z C • •
	Zero Page	LDX Oper	2	A6	
	Zero Page.Y	LDX Oper.Y	2	B6	
	Absolute	LDX Oper	3	AE	
	Absolute.Y	LDX Oper.Y	3	BE	
LDY Load index Y with memory	Immediate	LDY #Oper	2	A0	N V - B D I Z C • •
	Zero Page	LDY Oper	2	A4	
	Zero Page.X	LDY Oper.X	2	B4	
	Absolute	LDY Oper	3	AC	
	Absolute.X	LDY Oper.X	3	BC	

Name Description	Addressing Mode	Assembly Language Form	No Bytes	HEX OP Code	Status Register
LSR Shift right one bit (memory or accumulator) `0→[7 8 6 4 3 2 1 0]→C`	Accumulator Zero Page Zero Page.X Absolute Absolute.X	LSR A LSR Oper LSR Oper.X LSR Oper LSR Oper.X	1 2 2 3 3	4A 46 56 4E 5E	N V - B D I Z C 0 • •
NOP No operation	Implied	NOP	1	EA	N V - B D I Z C
ORA "OR" memory with accumulator	Immediate Zero Page Zero Page.X Absolute Absolute.X Absolute.Y (Indirect.X) (Indirect).Y	ORA #Oper ORA Oper ORA Oper.X ORA Oper ORA Oper.X ORA Oper.Y ORA (Oper.X) ORA (Oper).Y	2 2 2 3 3 3 2 2	09 05 15 0D 1D 19 01 11	N V - B D I Z C • •
PHA Push accumulator on stack	Implied	PHA	1	48	N V - B D I Z C
PHP Push processor status on stack	Implied	PHP	1	08	N V - B D I Z C
PLA Pull accumulator from stack	Implied	PLA	1	68	N V - B D I Z C • •
PLP Pull processor status from stack	Implied	PLP	1	28	N V - B D I Z C • • • • • • • •
ROL Rotate one bit left (memory or accumulator) `[7 6 5 4 3 2 1 0]←C←`	Accumulator Zero Page Zero Page.X Absolute Absolute.X	ROL A ROL Oper ROL Oper.X ROL Oper ROL Oper.X	1 2 2 3 3	2A 26 36 2E 3E	N V - B D I Z C • • •
ROR Rotate one bit right (memory or accumulator) `C→[7 6 5 4 3 2 1 0]→`	Accumulator Zero Page Zero Page.X Absolute Absolute.X	ROR A ROR Oper ROR Oper.X ROR Oper ROR Oper.X	1 2 2 3 3	6A 66 76 6E 7E	N V - B D I Z C • • •
RTI Return from interrupt	Implied	RTI	1	40	N V - B D I Z C • • • • • • • •
RTS Return from subroutine	Implied	RTS	1	60	N V - B D I Z C

Name Description	Addressing Mode	Assembly Language Form	No Bytes	HEX OP Code	Status Register
SBC Subtract memory from accumulator with borrow	Immediate Zero Page Zero Page.X Absolute Absolute.X Absolute.Y (Indirect.X) (Indirect).Y	SBC #Oper SBC Oper SBC Oper.X SBC Oper SBC Oper.X SBC Oper.Y SBC (Oper.X) SBC (Oper).Y	2 2 2 3 3 3 2 2	E9 E5 F5 ED FD F9 E1 F1	N V - B D I Z C • • • •
SEC Set carry flag	Implied	SEC	1	38	N V - B D I Z C 1
SED Set decimal mode	Implied	SED	1	F8	N V - B D I Z C 1
SEI Set interrupt disable status	Implied	SEI	1	78	N V - B D I Z C 1
STA Store accumulator in memory	Zero Page Zero Page.X Absolute Absolute.X Absolute.Y (Indirect.X) (Indirect).Y	STA Oper STA Oper.X STA Oper STA Oper.X STA Oper.Y STA (Oper.X) STA (Oper).Y	2 2 3 3 3 2 2	85 95 8D 9D 99 81 91	N V - B D I Z C
STX Store index X in memory	Zero Page Zero Page.Y Absolute	STX Oper STX Oper.Y STX Oper	2 2 3	86 96 8E	N V - B D I Z C
STY Store index Y in memory	Zero Page Zero Page.X Absolute	STY Oper STY Oper.X STY Oper	2 2 3	84 94 8C	N V - B D I Z C
TAX Transfer accumulator to index X	Implied	TAX	1	AA	N V - B D I Z C • •
TAY Transfer accumulator to index Y	Implied	TAY	1	A8	N V - B D I Z C • •
TSX Transfer stack pointer to index X	Implied	TSX	1	BA	N V - B D I Z C • •
TXA Transfer index X to accumulator	Implied	TXA	1	BA	N V - B D I Z C • •
TXS Transfer index X to stack pointer	Implied	TXS	1	9A	N V - B D I Z C
TYA Transfer index Y to accumulator	Implied	TYA	1	98	N V - B D I Z C • •

6502 MICROPROCESSOR OPERATION CODES
IN NUMERICAL VALUE ORDER

00 — BRK	2F — ???	5E — LSR — Sbsolute.X
01 — ORA — (Indirect.X)	30 — BMI	5F — ???
02 — ???	31 — AND — (Indirect).Y	60 — RTS
03 — ???	32 — ???	61 — ADC — (Indirect.X)
04 — ???	33 — ???	62 — ???
05 — ORA — Zero Page	34 — ???	63 — ???
06 — ASL — Zero Page	35 — AND — Zero Page.X	64 — ???
07 — ???	36 — ROL —Zero Page.X	65 — ACD — Zero Page
08 — PHP	37 — ???	66 — ROR — Zero Page
09 — ORA — Immediate	38 — SEC	67 — ???
0A — ASL — Accumulator	39 — AND — Absolute.Y	68 — PLA
0B — ???	3A — ???	69 — ADC — Immediate
0C — ???	3B — ???	6A — ROR — Accumulator
0D — ORA — Absolute	3C — ???	6B — ???
0E — ASL — Absolute	3D — AND — Absolute.X	6C — JMP — Indirect
0F — ???	3E — ROL — Absolute.X`	6D — ADC — Absolute
10 — BPL	3F — NOP	6E — ROR — Absolute
11 — ORA — (Indirect).Y	40 — RTI	6F — ???
12 — ???	41 — EOR — (Indirect.X)	70 — BVS
13 — ???	42 — ???	71 — ADC — (Indirect).Y
14 — ???	43 — ???	72 — ???
15 — ORA — Zero Page.X	44 — ???	73 — ???
16 — ASL — Zero Page.X	45 — EOR — Zero Page	74 — ???
17 — ???	46 — LSR – Zero Page	75 — ADC — Zero Page.X
18 — CLC	47 — ???	76 — ROR — Zero Page.X
19 — ORA — Absolute.Y	48 — PHA	77 — ???
1A — ???	49 — EOR — Immediate	78 — SEI
1B — ???	4A — LSR — Accumulator	79 — ADC — Absolute.Y
1C — ???	4B — ???	7A — ???
1D — ORA — Absolute.X	4C — JMP — Absolute	7B — ???
1E — ASL — Absolute.X	4D — EOR — Absolute	7C — ???
1F — ???	4E — LSR — Absolute	7D — ADC — Absolute.X
20 — JSR	4F — ???	7E — ROR — Absolute.X
21 — AND — (Indirect.X)	50 — BVC	7F — ???
22 — ???	51 — EOR (Indirect).Y	80 — ???
23 — ???	52 — ???	81 — STA — (Indirect.X)
24 — BIT — Zero Page	53 — ???	82 — ???
25 — AND — Zero Page	54 — ???	83 — ???
26 — ROL — Zero Page	55 — EOR — Zero Page.X	84 — STY — Zero Page
27 — ???	56 — LSR — Zero Page.X	85 — STA — Zero Page
28 — PLP	57 — ???	86 — STX — Zero Page
29 — AND — Immediate	58 — CLI	87 — ???
2A — ROL — Accumulator	59 — EOR — Absolute.Y	88 — DEY
2B — ???	5A — ???	89 — ???
2C — BIT — Absolute	5B — ???	8A — TXA
2D — AND — Absolute	5C — ???	8B — ???
2E — ROL — Absolute	5D — EOR — Absolute.X	8C — STY — Absolute

8D — STA — Absolute	B4 — LDY — Zero Page.X	DB — ???
8E — STX — Absolute	B5 — LDA — Zero Page.X	DC — ???
8F — ???	B6 — LDX — Zero Page. Y	DD — CMP — Absolute.X
90 — BCC	B7 — ???	DE — DEC — Absolute.X
91 — STA — (Indirect).Y	B8 — CLV	DF —
92 — ???	B9 — LDA — Absolute.Y	E0 - - CPX — Immediate
93 — ???	BA — TSX	E1 — SBC — (Indirect.X)
94 — STY — Zero Page.X	BB — ???	E2 — ???
95 — STA — Zero Page.X	BC — LDY — Absolute.X	E3 — ???
96 — STX — Zero Page.Y	BD — LDA — Absolute.X	E4 — CPX — Zero Page
97 — ???	BE — LDX — Absolute.Y	E5 — SBC — Zero Page
98 — TYA	BF — ???	E6 — INC — Zero Page
99 — STA — Absolute.Y	C0 — CPY — Immediate	E7 — ???
9A — TXS	C1 — CMP — (Indirect.X)	E8 — INX
9B — ???	C2 — ???	E9 — SBC — Immediate
9C — ???	C3 — ???	EA — NOP
9D — STA — Absolute.X	C4 — CPY — Zero Page	EB — ???
9E — ???	C5 — CMP — Zero Page	EC — CPX — Absolute
9F — ???	C6 — DEC — Zero Page	ED — SBC — Absolute
A0 — LDY — Immediate	C7 — ???	EE — INC — Absolute
A1 — LDA — (Indirect.X)	C8 — INY	EF — ???
A2 — LDX — Immediate	C9 — CMP — Immediate	F0 — BEQ
A3 — ???	CA — DEX	F1 — SBC — (Indirect).Y
A4 — LDY — Zero Page	CB — ???	F2 — ???
A5 — LDA — Zero Page	CC — CPY — Absolute	F3 — ???
A6 — LDX — Zero Page	CD — CMP — Absolute	F4 — ???
A7 — ???	CE — DEC — Absolute	F5 — SBC — Zero Page.X
A8 — TAY	CF — ???	F6 — INC — Zero Page.X
A9 — LDA — Immediate	D0 — BNE	F7 — ???
AA — TAX	C1 — CMP — (Indirect).Y	F8 — SED
AB — ???	D2 — ???	F9 — SBC — Absolute.Y
AC — LDY — Absolute	D3 — ???	FA — ???
AD — LDA — Absolute	D4 — ???	FB — ???
AE — LDX — Absolute	D5 — CMP — Zero Page.X	FC — ???
AF — ???	D6 — DEC — Zero Page.X	FD — SBC — Absolute.X
B0 — BCS	D7 — ???	FE — INC — Absolute.X
B1 — LDA — (Indirect).Y	D8 — CLD	FF — ???
B2 — ???	D9 — CMP — Absolute.Y	
B3 — ???	DA — ???	

???Undefined Operation

120

Appendix 2
Hexadecimal to Decimal Conversion Table

This table can be used to convert up to four digit hex numbers to decimal.

How to use the table:

1. Divide the number into groups of two digits,
   e.g. $F17B → F1   7B
         $2A   → 2A

2. Take the low byte of the number (from above 7B or 2A) and look it up in the chart. Find the most significant digit (7) in the column on the left, find the least significant digit (8) in the row along the top, and find the box in which the row (7) and the column (B) cross. In that box you will find 2 numbers, 123 31488 . These are the values of 7B in the low byte and the high byte. Since we are looking up the low byte, take the value 123. Now find the location of the high byte of our number (F1) on the chart. The box here contains 241 61696 . Since we are now dealing with the high byte, take the value 61696 from that box and add it to the value we found earlier for the low byte 123.

   61696
   + 123
   ———————
   61819   which is the decimal value of $F17B
   ———————

NOTE: to find the decimal value of a two digit number, e.g. 2A, look it up in the chart taking the low byte value (42). For a one digit number, e.g. E, create a two digit number by adding a leading zero (ØE), and similarly make three digit numbers four digits with a leading zero.

121

HEXADECIMAL TO DECIMAL CONVERSION TABLE LEAST SIGNIFICANT DIGIT

MOST SIGNIFICANT DIGIT

HEX	0 Low	0 High	1 Low	1 High	2 Low	2 High	3 Low	3 High	4 Low	4 High	5 Low	5 High	6 Low	6 High	7 Low	7 High	8 Low	8 High	9 Low	9 High	A Low	A High	B Low	B High	C Low	C High	D Low	D High	E Low	E High	F Low	F High
0	0	0	1	256	2	512	3	768	4	1024	5	1280	6	1536	7	1792	8	2048	9	2304	10	2560	11	2816	12	3072	13	3328	14	3584	15	3840
1	16	4096	17	4352	18	4608	19	4864	20	5120	21	5376	22	5632	23	5888	24	6144	25	6400	26	6656	27	6912	28	7168	29	7424	30	7680	31	7936
2	32	8192	33	8448	34	8704	35	8960	36	9216	37	9472	38	9728	39	9984	40	10240	41	10496	42	10752	43	11008	44	11264	45	11520	46	11776	47	12032
3	48	12288	49	12544	50	12800	51	13056	52	13312	53	13568	54	13824	55	14080	56	14336	57	14592	58	14848	59	15104	60	15360	61	15616	62	15872	63	16128
4	64	16384	65	16640	66	16896	67	17152	68	17408	69	17664	70	17920	71	18176	72	18432	73	18688	74	18944	75	19200	76	19456	77	19712	78	19968	79	20224
5	80	20480	81	20736	82	20992	83	21248	84	21504	85	21760	86	22016	87	22272	88	22528	89	22784	90	23040	91	23296	92	23552	93	23808	94	24064	95	24320
6	96	24576	97	24832	98	25088	99	25344	100	25600	101	25856	102	26112	103	26368	104	26624	105	26880	106	27136	107	27392	108	27648	109	27904	110	28160	111	28416
7	112	28672	113	28928	114	29184	115	29440	116	29696	117	29952	118	30208	119	30464	120	30720	121	30976	122	31232	123	31488	124	31744	125	32000	126	32256	127	32512
8	128	32768	129	33024	130	33280	131	33536	132	33792	133	34048	134	34304	135	34560	136	34816	137	35072	138	35328	139	35584	140	35840	141	36096	142	36352	143	36608
9	144	36864	145	37120	146	37376	147	37632	148	37888	149	38144	150	38400	151	38656	152	38912	153	39168	154	39424	155	39680	156	39936	157	40192	158	40448	159	40704
A	160	40960	161	41216	162	41472	163	41728	164	41984	165	42240	166	42496	167	42752	168	43008	169	43264	170	43520	171	43776	172	44032	173	44288	174	44544	175	44800
B	176	45056	177	45312	178	45568	179	45824	180	46080	181	46336	182	46592	183	46848	184	47104	185	47360	186	47616	187	47872	188	48128	189	48384	190	48640	191	48896
C	192	49152	193	49408	194	49664	195	49920	196	50176	197	50432	198	50688	199	50944	200	51200	201	51456	202	51712	203	51968	204	52224	205	52480	206	52736	207	52992
D	208	53248	209	53504	210	53760	211	54016	212	54272	213	54528	214	54784	215	55040	216	55296	217	55552	218	55808	219	56064	220	56320	221	56576	222	56832	223	57088
E	224	57344	225	57600	226	57856	227	58112	228	58368	229	58624	230	58880	231	59136	232	59392	233	59648	234	59904	235	60160	236	60416	237	60672	238	60928	239	61184
F	240	61440	241	61696	242	61952	243	62208	244	62464	245	62720	246	62976	247	63232	248	63488	249	63744	250	64000	251	64256	252	64512	253	64768	254	65024	255	65280

Appendix 3
Relative Branch and Two's Complement Numbering Tables

To calculate relative branches, locate the address immediately after the location of the branch instruction. Count the number of bytes from there to where you want the branch to end up. If the destination is before the first byte, use the backward branch table and if not, use the forward branch table. Look up the displacement(the number you counted) in the body of the appropriate chart and read off the high and low digits of the branch from the sides. This can also be used in reverse, by looking up a branch on the sides to find the displacement taken in the body of the chart.

To convert from a signed decimal number between −128 and 127 to a hex two's complement number, find your decimal number in the body of the appropriate chart(positives and negatives) and read off the hex two's complement number from the sides(high digit, low digit). The reverse process (two's complement hex to signed decimal) is simply a matter of finding the high digit on the column on the left, the low digit on the top row, reading off the number where the row and column meet, and if in the negative chart make the number negative.

FORWARD RELATIVE BRANCH **POSITIVE NUMBERS**

low\hi	0	1	2	3	4	5	6	7	8	9	A	B	C	D	E	F
0	0	1	2	3	4	5	6	7	8	9	10	11	12	13	14	15
1	16	17	18	19	20	21	22	23	24	25	26	27	28	29	30	31
2	32	33	34	35	36	37	38	39	40	41	42	43	44	45	46	47
3	48	49	50	51	52	53	54	55	56	57	58	59	60	61	62	63
4	64	65	66	67	68	69	70	71	72	73	74	75	76	77	78	79
5	80	81	82	83	84	85	86	87	88	89	90	91	92	93	94	95
6	96	97	98	99	100	101	102	103	104	105	106	107	108	109	110	111
7	112	113	114	115	116	117	118	119	120	121	122	123	124	125	126	127

BACKWARD RELATIVE BRANCH **NEGATIVE NUMBERS**

low\hi	0	1	2	3	4	5	6	7	8	9	A	B	C	D	E	F
8	128	127	126	125	124	123	122	121	120	119	118	117	116	115	114	113
9	112	111	110	109	108	107	106	105	104	103	102	101	100	99	98	97
A	96	95	94	93	92	91	90	89	88	87	86	85	84	83	82	81
B	80	79	78	77	76	75	74	73	72	71	70	69	68	67	66	65
C	64	63	62	61	60	59	58	57	56	55	54	53	52	51	50	49
D	48	47	46	45	44	43	42	41	40	39	38	37	36	35	34	33
E	32	31	30	29	28	27	26	25	24	23	22	21	20	19	18	17
F	16	15	14	13	12	11	10	9	8	7	6	5	4	3	2	1

Appendix 4
Atari 130XE Memory Map

$0000	$00FF	ZERO PAGE	$D000	$D0FF	GTIA CHIP
$0100	$01FF	STACK	$D100	$DFFF	SHADOW MEMORY
$0200	$05FF	VARIABLES USED BY BASIC AND O.S.	$D200	$D2FF	POKEY CHIP
			$D400	$D5FF	ANTIC CHIP
$0600	$06FF	SPARE MEMORY	$D600	$D7FF	SHADOW MEMORY
$0700	$07FF	USER BOOT AREA			
$07EC	$9C1F	BASIC PROGRAM AREA	$D800	$DFFF	FLOATING POINT ROM PACKAGE
$9C20	$9C3F	TEXT ZERO DISPLAY LIST	$E000	$E3FF	ATARI CHARACTER SET
$9C40	$9FFE	SCREEN MEMORY IN MODE ZERO	$E400	$E44F	DEVICE VECTOR TABLE
$A000	$BFFF	ATARI BASIC INTERPRETER	$E44F	$FFFF	OPERATING SYSTEM ROM
$C000	$CFFF	UNUSED MEMORY SPACE			END OF MEMORY

Appendix 5
The Screen Chip

The ATARI's screen is controlled by two very powerful chips, the GTIA and the ANTIC chip. These chips generate background, foreground, color information, process shape data, missiles, and players. The Antic chip is really a simple programmable microprocessor with it's own individual instruction set. The GTIA chip handles the generation and movement of players and missiles. This chip is controlled primarly by the ANTIC chip. It extends in memory from $D000 to $D0FF. GTIA stands for George's television interface adapter. Here is a list of the memory locations associated with the GTIA chip and the functions they perform.

GTIA Chip

$D000-$D003

These registers perform a dual function, they control the horizontal position of players 0 to 3 and also indicate with what playfield a player has collided. Writing to these registers invokes the first function and reading from them the second. Poking data into these registers will move a player in the horizontal position across the screen. It is possible to put any value between 0 and 255 into a register however for the player to be visible it must in the range 48 to 208. Otherwise it will be under the screen border rendering it invisible. These values will alter from television to television.The register at $D000 is for player 0 and so on upwards.

$D004-$D007

These registers perform an identical task to the ones above except that they act on the missiles instead of the players. As above, the register at $D004 is for missile zero and so on upward.

$D008-$D00B

A player can be set to one of three sizes by placing a value in these registers. The sizes available are normal, double and

quadruple. These size increases are achieved by doubling and
quadrupling the width of the pixels in the player. Putting a
zero will set the player to normal size, a one will double his
size and a three will quadruple it. Reading these registers
indicates whether a missile to player collision has occurred.

$DØØC

This register sets the size of all four missiles. A missile is
two pixels wide and like players can be either normal, double
or quadruple size. This register contains eight bits and two
bits are assigned to each missile to set the size. Here is a
table which explains how to set the various bits in the
register to expand the missile.

Missile	bits-to-set	x1	x2	x4
Ø	Ø & 1	2	1	3
1	2 & 3	8	4	12
2	4 & 5	32	16	48
3	6 & 7	128	64	192

Reading this register will indicate whether a Player Ø to
player collision has occurred.

$DØØD-$DØ1Ø

Writing to these registers enables the ANTIC chip to be
effectively bypassed. Normally when a player is displayed on
the screen the shape data to be displayed is fetched from an
area of RAM automatically by a process called DMA. This
process can be switched off and the data fetched from this
register instead. The limitation is that only one byte of
shape data can be displayed down the whole length of the
player. Writing to these registers will control players Ø to
3. Reading from $DØØD to $DØØF will determine whether there
has been a collision between players 1-3 and another player.
Reading from $DØ1Ø will signal whether joystick trigger Ø has
been pressed. Normally PEEKing from this register will return
a one but when joystick zero is pressed the location will go to
zero.

$DØ11

This location works the same as the one above except that it
works with missiles and only one register is needed to control
four missiles. Only bit pairs are assigned to each missile
because a missile is two bits wide. The bit pairs that go with
the missiles can be found in the following table:

Missile number	bit pairs
Ø	Ø & 1
1	2 & 3
2	4 & 5
3	6 & 7

Reading this location will give the input at joystick one. As with joystick zero normally this location will output a one and holding down joystick one will cause it to go to zero.

$DØ12-$DØ15

These locations control the color and luminances of players Ø and 1. Normally a missile will be the same color as it's associate player. However if the four missiles are merged together to form a fifth player they take on their own individual color. Reading from location $DØ14 will determine what kind of television system is implemented, PAL or NTSC. If the bits 1-3 equal zero then the system is PAL otherwise if the bits are 1 then the system is running NTSC.

$DØ16-$DØ19

These registers set the color and luminace of of playfields zero to three.

$DØ1A

This register sets the color and luminance of the background.

$DØ1D

Used to select players, missiles and latch trigger input. Bit Ø is used to turn on missiles, bit 1 is for players and bit 2 latches the trigger inputs. By setting this location to zero all players and missiles are switched off.

$DØ1E

Writing to this register will clear all collision registers of players and missiles.

$DØ1F

Reading from this location will indicate which of the three keys OPTION, SELECT and START are being pressed. Normally when this location is read a seven is returned but pressing one of these keys will switch off a bit. START is bit Ø, SELECT is bit 1 and OPTION is bit 2.

127

The ANTIC chip

The screen display is generated by the ANTIC chip which unlike
conventional video processors is programmable. ANTIC has it's
own instruction set and it is only necessary to put the program
in memory and point ANTIC at it. The list of instructions
which controls the ANTIC chip are called the display list.
Unlike a full microprocessor however the instruction set is
extremely simple. The different options are selected by
setting the right bits in the instruction. There are four
basic options in the instructions. They are Display list
Interupts, load memory scan, the vertical and horizontal scroll
registers.

A display list interrupt is invoked by setting bit 7 of an
instruction. When ANTIC comes to execute one of these
instructions it will cause an interrupt to occur. A load
memory scan tells ANTIC that the next two bytes following are
where the text screen memory is positioned. Normally these two
bytes will hold 40000 in LSB/MSB format. This mode is invoked
by setting bit 6 of the instruction. Setting bit 5 of an
instruction will enable fine vertical scrolling and setting bit
4 will enable fine horizontal scrolling. Setting these two
bits only enables fine scrolling it doesn't actually cause it.
Bits 0 to 3 are used to specify the graphics mode wanted. The
ANTIC modes are functionally identical to BASIC graphics modes
but just numbered differently.

Here is the display list that is normally found in BASIC text
mode 0.

DECIMAL	HEX	DECIMAL	HEX
112	70	2	02
112	70	2	02
112	70	2	02
66	42	2	02
64	40	2	02
156	9C	2	02
2	02	2	02
2	02	2	02
2	02	2	02
2	02	2	02
2	02	2	02
2	02	2	02
2	02	2	02
2	02	65	41
2	02	32	20
2	02	156	9C

The three 112's at the start of the display list put a border
at the top of the screen otherwise the screen would be jittery
or would roll. The 66 tells ANTIC that the two bytes following
are the address of the screen memory. Normally in graphic mode
Ø the screen is located at 4ØØØØ decimal (4ØØØØ=156*256+64),
though in actually fact the screen can live any where. Notice
the bits which are set in the instruction, bit 6 to signify a
load memory instruction and bit 1 to indicate ANTIC mode 2 or
BASIC's graphic mode zero. The 23 bytes that follow are all
twos and indicate that each line is to be in ANTIC mode two,
which corrosponds to BASIC mode Ø. It was not necessary to set
load memory because this had already been done. The 65 told
ANTIC to jump back to the start of the display list and to use
the following two bytes as an address.

There are two kinds of JMP instructions in ANTIC: JMP straight
to the address specified in the following two bytes and JMP
when a vertical blank is occurring. A pointer to the display
list can be found by:

    PRINT PEEK(56Ø)+PEEK(561)*256

Here is a list of the modes available with ANTIC:

ANTIC MODE	No-COLORS	BYTES/SCREEN
2	2	96Ø
3	2	76Ø
4	4	96Ø
5	4	48Ø
6	5	48Ø
7	5	24Ø
8	4	24Ø
9	2	48Ø
1Ø	4	96Ø
11	2	192Ø
12	2	384Ø
13	4	384Ø
14	4	768Ø
15	2	768Ø

0 GRAY	4 PINK	8 BLUE	12 GREEN
1 GOLD	5 PURPLE	9 LIGHT BLUE	13 YELLOW-GREEN
2 ORANGE	6 RED-ORANGE	10 TURQUOISE	14 ORANGE-GREEN
3 RED-ORANGE	7 BLUE	11 GREEN-BLUE	15 LIGHT-ORANGE

TABLE OF COLOR VALUES

Appendix 6
The Sound Chip

Sound on the ATARI is generated by a chip called POKEY. This chip serves a multitude of other purposes including scanning the keyboard, random number seed, communication with serial devices and the interrupt source. The POKEY chip lives at addresses $D2ØØ to $D2FF. In actual fact only locations $D2ØØ to $D2ØF are used, the rest of this page is a set of duplicates of the first sixteen bytes. Because the POKEY chip controls the disk drive and tape recorder (and all serial bus activity), it will need to be initialized after any of these devices are used.

The sound chip has four independant voices. It is possible to set the frequency of a note, the volume and the amount of noise. The sound chip is selected in machine language by storing zero at $D2Ø8 and 3 at $D2ØF.

There is a frequency register for each of the four voices. It is not a frequency register in the conventional sense. Instead of loading a frequency into this register, you load a value that you want the sound chips input clock frequency divided by. So the greater the number, the lower the frequency of the voice. So if a four is loaded in one of these registers, then for every four ticks of the sound clock a pulse will be output. The four frequency registers are located at $D2ØØ, $D2Ø2, $D2Ø4 and $D2Ø6.

Again for each of the voices there is special control register for volume and distortion (noise). These registers can be found at locations $D2Ø1, $D2Ø3, $D2Ø5 and $D2Ø7. Bits zero to four control the volume level of a voice and bits five to seven the distortion level. A zero volume is achieved by putting zero in the bottom four bits and the loudest volume by putting in 15. Adding together the volumes of all the voices must not result in a number greater than 32 or there will be buzzing.

The ATARI does not have distortion in the real sense. Distortion in the proper sense is generated by tugging at the waveforms in a controlled manner. On the ATARI it's achieved by simply removing pulses from the square waveform according to

which distortion is chosen. This is really noise. Distortion
is generated from three special counters called poly-counters.
Setting the upper three bits in the control registers selects
the poly-counter to be used. The three poly-counters are four,
five and seventeen bits long.
Here is a table of bit values to put in the control registers
and the poly-counters combinations they will select.   An   X   in
any of the bit positions means that it is irrelevant what value
that position takes on.

BITS
7 6 5

Ø Ø Ø -divide input clock by frequency, use 5 bit and 17 bit
poly-counters and divide by two.

Ø X 1 -divide input clock by frequency, use 5 bit poly-counter
and divide by two.

Ø 1 Ø -divide input clock by frequency, use 5 and 4 bit
poly-counters and divide by two.

1 Ø Ø -divide input clock by frequency, use 17 bit
poly-counter and divide by two.

1 X 1 -divide input clock by frequency and divide by two.

1 1 Ø -divide input clock by frequency, use 4 bit poly-counter
and divide by two.

At $D2Ø8 there is a control register that works on on all four
voices. Each of the bits in this location perform a particular
task. Here is a list of the tasks that each of the bits
perform:

Bit Ø -switches the clock input between 64 KHz and 15 KHz.

Bit 1 -places a filter into channel two and clock it with voice
four.

Bit 2 -places a filter into channel one and clock it with voice
three.

Bit 3 -fuse frequency registers of voices four and three and
use as sixteen bit frequency register.

Bit 4 -fuse frequency registers of voices two and one and use
as sixteen bit frequency register.

Bit 5 -use the 1.79 MHz system clock as an input to the sound
chip on voice three.

Bit 6 —use the 1.79 MHz system clock as an input to the sound chip on voice one.

Bit 7 —set the 17 bitpoly-counter to a 9 bit poly-counter.

This location is very important for controlling the input frequencies of the voices. It is possible to set the frequencies to 1.79 Mhz (the system clock), 64 KHz and 15 KHz. Do this using by changing bits Ø, 5 and 6. This greatly expands the range of achievable notes. Another method of expanding frequency range is to increase the size of the number that you divide into the main input frequency. Normally the number divided into the frequency is in the range Ø-255 but this can be expanded to 65535 by changing bits 3 and 4.

Appendix 7
Memory Usage Directory

<pre>
PAGE ZERO
ADDRESS   DECIMAL   DESCRIPTION
(HEX)

ØØØØ ØØØ1   Ø-1   Vblank timer value
ØØØ2 ØØØ3   2-3   Cassette jump vector
ØØØ4 ØØØ5   4-5   Pointer to disk boot address
ØØØ6   6   Temporary size of RAM
ØØØ7   7   Cartridge B insert flag
ØØØ8   8   Warmstart flag
ØØØ9   9   Good boot flag
ØØØA ØØØB   1Ø-11   Disk boot vector
ØØØC ØØØD   12-13   Init pointer for disk boot
ØØØE ØØØF   14-15   Pointer to top of memory
ØØ1Ø   16   Shadow for POKEY enable
ØØ11   17   Break key pressed Ø=pressed
ØØ12 ØØ14   18-2Ø   Realtime clock
ØØ15 ØØ16   21-22   Pointer to disk buffer
ØØ17   23   CIO command
ØØ18 ØØ19   24-25   Pointer to disk manager
ØØ1A ØØ1B   26-27   Pointer to disk utilities
ØØ1C   28   Printer timeout value
ØØ1D   29   Points to position in printer buff
ØØ1E   3Ø   Size of printer line
ØØ1F   31   Character being output.
ØØ2Ø   32   Handler index
ØØ21   33   The current device number
ØØ22   34   Command byte
ØØ23   35   Result of last I/O operation
ØØ24 ØØ25   36-37   Pointer to data buffer
ØØ26 ØØ27   38-39   Pointer to put byte routine
ØØ28 ØØ29   4Ø-41   Count for buffer count
ØØ2A   42   Type of file access flag
ØØ2B   43   Used by serial bus routines
ØØ2C ØØ2D   44-45   Used by NOTE and POINT
ØØ2E   46   Byte being accessed in sector
ØØ2F   47   Temporary storage for char in PUT
ØØ3Ø   48   Status of current serial operation
ØØ31   49   Checksum for serial bus operation
ØØ32 ØØ33   5Ø-51   Pointer to serial data buffer
</pre>

0034 0035	52-53	Pointer past previous buffer
0036	54	Number of times to retry I/O operation
0037	55	Number of device present retries
0038	56	Indicates buffer is full, 255=full
003D	61	Pointer to cassette pointer
003E	62	Type of gap between records
003F	63	Flag to indicate end of cass file
0040	64	Beep count
0041	65	Noise flag, used to switch off I/O noise
0042	66	Flag to indicate Time critical I/O
0043 0049	67-73	File manager zero page variables.
004A	74	Boot flag for cassette
004B	75	Flag to indicate disk and cassette boot
004C	76	Break abort status
004D	77	Color attract flag
0050 0051	80-81	Temporary register
0052	82	Left margin of display
0053	83	Right margin of display
0054	84	Current row number
0055 0056	85-86	Current column number
0057	87	Display mode
0058 0059	88-89	Pointer to start of screen memory
005A	90	Old cursor row
005B 005C	91-92	Old cursor column
005D	93	Value of character under cursor
005E 005F	94-95	Pointer to current cursor position
0060	96	Row pointer to DRAWTO point
0061 0062	97-98	Column pointer to DRAWTO point
0063	99	Position of cursor in logical line
0064 0069	100-105	Temporary information
006A 006B	106	Page number of RAM top
006B	107	Character count in screen line
006C 006D	108-109	Pointer to editor getchar routine
006E	110	Temporary storage
006F	111	Justification counter
0070 0073	112-115	Tempory registers for plotting
0074 007A	116-122	Registers for line drawing
007B	123	Split screen flag
007C	124	Storage for character from keyboard
007D	125	Temporary storage
007E 007F	126-127	Number of points to draw line
0080 0081	128-129	Pointer to start of Basic low memory
0082 0083	130-131	Pointer to variable name list
0084 0085	132-133	Pointer to end of variable name list
0086 0087	134-135	Pointer to variable data values
0088 0089	136-137	Pointer to start of BASIC program
008A 008B	138-139	Pointer to currently executing statement
008C 008D	140-141	Pointer to end of BASIC program
008E 008F	142-143	Pointer to GOSUB/FOR/NEXT stack
0090 0091	144-145	Pointer to top of memory used by BASIC

```
0092 00B0    146-202    Used by BASIC ROM
00BA 00BB    186-187    Linenumber  where program stopped
00C3         195        Error number of last error
00C9         201        Number of spaces between TAB columns
00CB 00D1    203-209    Spare bytes in zero page
00D2 00D3    210-211    Temporary location for calculations
00D4 00D9    212-217    Zero page,floating point accumulator 0
00E0 00E5    224-229    Second floating point accumulator
00E6 00F1    230-241    More floating point information
00F2         242        Index to character input buffer
00F3 00F4    243-244    Pointer line input buffer
00F5 00FF    245-255    Temporary floating point registers

PAGE ONE
0100 01FF    256-511    System stack
```

135

Appendix 8
Table of Screen Codes

NORMAL VIDEO

FOR THIS	TYPE THIS	FOR THIS	TYPE THIS	FOR THIS	TYPE THIS	FOR THIS	TYPE THIS
♥	CTRL ,	◣	CTRL J	●	CTRL T	←	ESC CTRL +
▶	CTRL A	◨	CTRL K	■	CTRL U	→	ESC CTRL *
▮	CTRL B	◪	CTRL L	▮	CTRL V	◆	CTRL .
◰	CTRL C	▬	CTRL M	▼	CTRL W	↑	CTRL ;
◀	CTRL D	▃	CTRL N	▲	CTRL X	│	SHIFT =
◥	CTRL E	▪	CTRL O	▮	CTRL Y	◤	ESC SHIFT CLEAR
◿	CTRL F	♣	CTRL P	◣	CTRL Z		
◺	CTRL G	◨	CTRL Q	€	ESC ESC	◀	ESC DELETE
◢	CTRL H	▬	CTRL R	↑	ESC CTRL −	▶	ESC TAB
▪	CTRL I	✚	CTRL S	↓	ESC CTRL =		

136

INVERSE VIDEO

FOR THIS ▼	TYPE THIS ▼	FOR THIS ▼	TYPE THIS ▼	FOR THIS ▼	TYPE THIS ▼
♥	⅄ CTRL ,	◼	⅄ CTRL O	⬇	ESC SHIFT INSERT
▮	⅄ CTRL A	⬙	⅄ CTRL P	➡	ESC CTRL TAB
▮	⅄ CTRL B	◪	⅄ CTRL Q	⬅	ESC SHIFT TAB
◩	⅄ CTRL C	▬	⅄ CTRL R	◆	⅄ CTRL .
◪	⅄ CTRL D	✛	⅄ CTRL S	⬢	⅄ CTRL ;
◪	⅄ CTRL E	◻	⅄ CTRL T	▮	⅄ SHIFT =
◿	⅄ CTRL F	▭	⅄ CTRL U	◤	ESC CTRL 2
◤	⅄ CTRL G	▮	⅄ CTRL V	◀	ESC CTRL DELETE
◥	⅄ CTRL H	⊤	⅄ CTRL W	▶	ESC CTRL
◻	⅄ CTRL I	⊥	⅄ CTRL X		
◥	⅄ CTRL J	▯	⅄ CTRL Y		
◻	⅄ CTRL K	◳	⅄ CTRL Z		
▣	⅄ CTRL L	⬆	ESC SHIFT DELETE		
▬	⅄ CTRL M				
▬	⅄ CTRL N				

137

Appendix 9
Current Key Pressed

Location 754 stores the last key pressed. Only one key may be pressed at a time and if two are pressed then the first one hit will register. This location holds the value of the hardware register read and not the actual ASCII value of the key pressed. This memory location is a shadow location. The value of the last key pressed will remain at this location until it is cleared by a POKE or another key is pressed. Here is a table of the values returned by PEEKing this location.

Key	Value	Key	Value	Key	Value	Key	Value
ESC	28	TAB	44	CTRL	NOTHING	SHIFT	NOTHING
1	31	Q	47	A	63	Z	23
2	3Ø	W	46	S	62	X	22
3	26	E	42	D	58	C	18
4	24	R	4Ø	F	56	V	16
5	29	T	45	G	61	B	21
6	27	Y	43	H	57	N	35
7	51	U	11	J	1	M	37
8	53	I	13	K	5	,	32
9	48	O	8	L	Ø	.	34
Ø	5Ø	P	1Ø	;	2	/	38
(	54	–	14	+	6	INVERS	39
)	55	=	15	*	7	SPACE	33
Bk sp	52	RETURN	12	CAPS	6Ø		

Appendix 10
ALPA + Disassembler

ALPA

```
10      CLR :GOSUB 1000
12      GOSUB 12000
20      GOSUB 1700:IF NL=1 THEN RETURN
30      PAS=1:FOR Z1=1 TO NL-1:GOSUB 2000:GOSUB 2500:GOSUB 3000:GO
        SUB 4000
70      IF TYPE=1 THEN GOSUB 5000
80      IF TYPE=2 THEN GOSUB 3500
90      GOSUB 7000:GOSUB 7500:NEXT Z1
200     REM PASS 2
205     NC=1
210     PAS=2:FOR Z1=1 TO NL-1:GOSUB 2000:GOSUB 2500:GOSUB 4000
225     IF TYPE=1 THEN GOSUB 5000
230     IF TYPE=2 THEN GOSUB 3500
235     GOSUB 7000:NEXT Z1
240     GOSUB 7600:RETURN
1000    REM INIT SYSTEM
1010    DIM LINE$(80),CODE$(3),INFOS$(20),OPER$(15),CHAR$(1),H$(16
        ),HZ$(4),EN1(100),ST1(100)
1012    DIM TEXT$(1000),PU$(40),MAND$(18),MOR$(18),A$(3),OTABLE$(8
        45),VA$(9),HX$(2),CH$(1),MEM$(6),DIRE$(12)
1015    OSIZE=15:NDIR=4:FG=100
1020    DIM HEX$(2),SYS$(10),SYMBOL$(220),LABEL$(10),LVALUE$(4),ME
        M(FG)
1030    H$="0123456789ABCDEF"
1035    NL=1:EPOIN=1:SYMBOL$(1,1)=CHR$(0)
1037    DIRE$="DFBDFWEQUORG"
1045    POIN=1:ST=1
1050    NMODE=11:FR=1
1060    INFOS$="▲▲▲▲▲▲▲▲▲▲▲▲▲▲▲▲▲▲▲▲"
1500    DATA 104,104,133,213,104,133,212
1510    DATA 104,37,213,133,213,104,37,212,133,212,96
1530    FOR I=1 TO 18:READ A:MAND$(I,I)=CHR$(A):NEXT I
1540    MOR$=MAND$:MOR$(9,9)=CHR$(5):MOR$(14,14)=CHR$(5)
1550    OTABLE$="▲":OTABLE$(840)="▲":OTABLE$(2,840)=OTABLE$(1,840-
        1)
1600    READ NOPS
1610    FOR I=1 TO 840 STEP OSIZE
1630    READ A$,ADDR,N:M1=INT(ADDR/256):L1=ADDR-(M1*256)
1650    OTABLE$(I,I+2)=A$:OTABLE$(I+3,I+3)=CHR$(L1):OTABLE$(I+4,I+
        4)=CHR$(M1)
1690    FOR J=1 TO N:READ A:OTABLE$(I+4+J,I+4+J)=CHR$(A):NEXT J:NE
        XT I
1699    RETURN
1700    REM INIT ASSEMBLER
1705    ST=1:PC=0:EPOIN=1:SYMBOL$(1,1)=CHR$(0):V=0:NC=1:SYSL=0
1710    FOR I=0 TO FG:MEM(I)=0:NEXT I
1999    RETURN
```

```
2000    REM INTIALIZE VARIABLES IN LINE
2005    LINE$="":LE=0:FLAG=0
2010    ERR=0:ADDR=0:INFOS$="":MEM$="▲▲"
2030    TYPE=0:CHAR$="":OPER$=""
2050    MODE=1:CODE$="▲▲":HX$="▲▲"
2055    PU$(1,40)="▲▲▲▲▲▲▲▲▲▲▲▲▲▲▲▲▲▲▲▲▲▲▲▲▲▲▲▲▲▲▲▲▲▲▲▲
        ▲▲▲▲"
2499    RETURN
2500    REM GET LINE
2505    ST1=ST1(Z1):EN1=EN1(Z1):JJ=1
2510    FOR J=ST1 TO EN1:LINE$(JJ,JJ)=TEXT$(J,J):JJ=JJ+1:NEXT J:CO
        UNT=(EN1-ST1)+2:RETURN
2999    RETURN
3000    REM PROCESS AN LABEL
3005    CC=1:SYSL=1:LE=LEN(LINE$)
3010    GOSUB 6500:IF CH$<>"▲" THEN SYS$(SYSL,SYSL)=CH$:SYSL=SYSL+
        1:GOTO 3010
3015    SYSL=SYSL-1:IF SYSL<>0 THEN FLAG=1
3020    RETURN
3500    REM ASSEMBLER DIRECTIVES
3502    OPER$=LINE$(16,LEN(LINE$)):OP=LEN(OPER$)
3505    IF CODE$="DFB" THEN 3550:RETURN
3510    IF CODE$="DFW" THEN 3650:RETURN
3515    IF CODE$="EQU" THEN 3700:RETURN
3520    IF CODE$="ORG" THEN 3750:RETURN
3550    REM DEFINE BYTE
3555    GOSUB 5300
3557    IF LEN(MEM$)<>2 THEN GOSUB 6010:RETURN
3559    HX$=MEM$(1,2):GOSUB 9000:M1=DEC
3560    GOSUB 9100:PU$(6,7)=MEM$(1,2):MEM(NC)=DEC
3565    PC=PC+1:NC=NC+1:GOSUB 9300:RETURN
3650    REM DEFINE WORD
3655    GOSUB 5300:GOSUB 9100
3660    PU$(6,7)=MEM$(3,4):PU$(9,10)=MEM$(1,2)
3665    HX$=MEM$(3,4):GOSUB 9000:MEM(NC)=DEC
3670    NC=NC+1:HX$=MEM$(1,2):GOSUB 9200:MEM(NC)=DEC:NC=NC+1:PC=PC
        +2:GOSUB 9300:RETURN
3700    REM PROCESS EQU
3701    IF PAS=2 THEN RETURN
3702    IF FLAG=0 THEN PRINT "LABEL▲WITHOUT▲EQU":ERR=1:RETURN
3705    GOSUB 5300:GOSUB 9300
3710    IF COUNT=2 THEN V=1:HX$=MEM$(1,2):GOSUB 9000:PG=DEC:GOSUB
        6600:RETURN
3715    IF COUNT=4 THEN V=2:HX$=MEM$(3,4):GOSUB 9000:L3=DEC:HX$=ME
        M$(1,2):GOSUB 9000:M3=DEC:PG=(M3*256)+L3:GOSUB 6600:RETURN

3720    GOSUB 6010:RETURN
3750    REM ORG
3755    GOSUB 5300:GOSUB 9300
3760    IF LEN(MEM$)<>4 THEN GOSUB 6010:RETURN
3765    HX$=MEM$(1,2):GOSUB 9000:M1=DEC
3767    HX$=MEM$(3,4):GOSUB 9000:L1=DEC
3770    PC=(M1*256)+L1:PC1=PC:GOSUB 9300:RETURN
4000    REM PROCESS OPERATION CODE
4015    CODE$=LINE$(8,10)
4020    FOR I=1 TO (NOPS*OSIZE) STEP OSIZE
4025    IF CODE$=OTABLE$(I,I+2) THEN INFOS$=OTABLE$(I,I+OSIZE-1):T
        YPE=1:RETURN
4030    NEXT I
4035    REM
4040    FOR I=1 TO (NDIR*3) STEP 3
```

140

```
4045    IF CODE$=DIRE$(I,I+2) THEN TYPE=2:RETURN
4047    NEXT I
4050    PRINT "UNKNOWN OPERATION CODE":ERR=1:RETURN
5000    REM PROCESS OPERAND
5005    IF FLAG=1 THEN V=2:PG=PC:GOSUB 6600
5010    IF LEN(LINE$)<16 THEN MODE=1:RETURN
5015    OPER$=LINE$(16,LEN(LINE$)):OP=LEN(OPER$)
5020    CHAR$=OPER$(1,1)
5025    IF CHAR$="(" THEN GOSUB 5100:RETURN
5030    IF CHAR$="#" THEN GOSUB 5200:RETURN
5035    IF CHAR$="$" THEN GOSUB 5300:RETURN
5037    IF CHAR$="&" THEN GOSUB 5400:RETURN
5040    A=ASC(CHAR$):IF A>=65 AND A<=90 THEN GOSUB 5500:RETURN
5095    GOSUB 6030:RETURN
5100    REM PROCESS INDIRECTION
5105    CC=2:GOSUB 5700
5107    IF CH$="$" THEN GOSUB 5150:RETURN
5108    A=ASC(CH$):IF A>=65 AND A<=90 THEN GOSUB 5600:RETURN
5110    GOSUB 6000:RETURN
5150    REM PROCESS HEX INDIRECTION
5151    COUNT=1
5152    GOSUB 5700:IF TR=1 THEN MEM$(COUNT,COUNT)=CH$:COUNT=COUNT+
        1:GOTO 5152
5153    COUNT=COUNT-1
5154    IF CH$="," THEN GOSUB 5160:RETURN
5156    IF CH$=")" THEN GOSUB 5170:RETURN
5157    GOSUB 6000:RETURN
5160    REM PROCESS INDIRECTION X
5161    IF COUNT<>2 THEN GOSUB 6000:RETURN
5162    GOSUB 5700:IF CH$<>"X" THEN GOSUB 6000:RETURN
5163    GOSUB 5700:IF CH$<>")" THEN GOSUB 6000:RETURN
5164    MODE=512:RETURN
5170    REM INDIRECT,Y OR (INDIRECT)
5171    IF COUNT=4 THEN GOSUB 5180:RETURN
5172    IF COUNT=2 THEN GOSUB 5190:RETURN
5173    GOSUB 6010:RETURN
5180    REM PROCESS ABSOLUTE INDIRECTION
5181    GOSUB 5700:IF CH$="" THEN MODE=1024:RETURN
5182    GOSUB 6000:RETURN
5190    REM PROCESS INDIRECT,Y
5191    GOSUB 5700:IF CH$<>"," THEN GOSUB 6000:RETURN
5192    GOSUB 5700:IF CH$<>"Y" THEN GOSUB 6000:RETURN
5193    GOSUB 5700:IF CH$<>"" THEN GOSUB 6000:RETURN
5194    MODE=256:RETURN
5200    REM PROCESS IMMEDIATE DATA
5205    MODE=2
5215    CHAR$=OPER$(2,2)
5220    IF CHAR$="$" THEN GOSUB 5250:RETURN
5225    GOSUB 6010:RETURN
5250    REM PROCESS IMMEDIATE HEX DATA
5255    HX$=OPER$(3,LEN(OPER$))
5260    IF LEN(HX$)>2 THEN GOSUB 6010:RETURN
5261    IF LEN(HX$)<2 THEN HX$(2,2)=HX$(1,1):HX$(1,1)="0":GOSUB 90
        00:IMM=DEC:RETURN
5265    GOSUB 9000:IMM=DEC:RETURN
5300    REM GENERATE HEX MEMORY OBJECT
5305    CC=2:COUNT=1
5310    GOSUB 5700:IF TR=1 THEN MEM$(COUNT,COUNT)=CH$:COUNT=COUNT+
        1:GOTO 5310
5315    COUNT=COUNT-1
5317    IF CH$="," THEN GOSUB 5750:RETURN
5319    IF CH$="" THEN GOSUB 5800:RETURN
```

141

```
5321  PRINT "ILLEGAL CHARACTER IN OPERAND":ERR=1:RETURN
5400  REM RELATIVE BRANCH
5401  CHAR$=OPER$(2,2)
5402  IF CHAR$="$" THEN GOSUB 5410:RETURN
5404  IF CHAR$>="A" AND CHAR$<="Z" THEN GOSUB 5450:RETURN
5406  GOSUB 6070:RETURN
5410  REM PROCESS HEX LABEL
5412  CC=3:COUNT=1
5414  GOSUB 5700:IF TR=1 THEN MEM$(COUNT,COUNT)=CH$:COUNT=COUNT+
      1:GOTO 5414
5415  COUNT=COUNT-1
5416  IF CH$<>"" THEN GOSUB 6010:RETURN
5419  MODE=2048:RETURN
5450  REM RELATIVE LABEL
5451  LABEL$(1,1)=CHAR$:LSIZE=2:CC=3
5453  GOSUB 6800:IF TR=1 THEN LABEL$(LSIZE,LSIZE)=CH$:LSIZE=LSIZ
      E+1:GOTO 5453
5455  LSIZE=LSIZE-1:GOSUB 6700
5457  IF FOUND=1 THEN MEM$=LVALUE$:GOSUB 5416:RETURN
5459  IF PAS=2 THEN GOSUB 6085:RETURN
5460  MEM$="0000":COUNT=4:GOSUB 5416:RETURN
5499  RETURN
5500  REM PROCESS LABEL IN OPERAND
5501  LABEL$(1,1)=CHAR$:LSIZE=2:CC=2
5503  GOSUB 6800:IF TR=1 THEN LABEL$(LSIZE,LSIZE)=CH$:LSIZE=LSIZ
      E+1:GOTO 5503
5505  LSIZE=LSIZE-1:GOSUB 6700
5515  IF FOUND=1 THEN MEM$=LVALUE$:GOSUB 5317:RETURN
5519  IF PAS=2 THEN GOSUB 6085:RETURN
5520  MEM$="0000":COUNT=4:GOSUB 5317:RETURN
5600  REM LABEL INDIRECTION
5601  LABEL$(1,1)=CH$:LSIZE=2:CC=3
5603  GOSUB 6800:IF TR=1 THEN LABEL$(LSIZE,LSIZE)=CH$:LSIZE=LSIZ
      E+1:GOTO 5603
5605  LSIZE=LSIZE-1:GOSUB 6700
5610  IF FOUND=1 THEN MEM$=LVALUE$:GOSUB 5154:RETURN
5612  IF PAS=2 THEN GOSUB 6085:RETURN
5615  MEM$="00":COUNT=2:GOSUB 5154:RETURN
5700  REM GET CHAR FROM OPERAND
5705  TR=0:CH$=""
5710  IF CC>OP THEN RETURN
5715  CH$=OPER$(CC,CC):CC=CC+1:A=ASC(CH$)
5720  IF A>=65 AND A<=70 THEN TR=1:RETURN
5730  IF A>=48 AND A<=57 THEN TR=1:RETURN
5735  RETURN
5750  REM PROCESS AN INDEX REGISTER
5755  GOSUB 5700
5760  IF CH$="X" THEN GOSUB 5780:RETURN
5765  IF CH$="Y" THEN GOSUB 5790:RETURN
5770  PRINT "ILLEGAL INDEX REGISTER FOLLOWING VALUE":ERR=1:RETUR
      N
5780  REM DETERMINE IF ZERO/ABSOLUTE X
5785  IF COUNT=2 THEN MODE=8:RETURN
5787  IF COUNT=4 THEN MODE=64:RETURN
5789  GOSUB 6010:RETURN
5790  REM DETERMINE IF ZERO/ABSOLUTE Y
5795  IF COUNT=2 THEN MODE=16:RETURN
5797  IF COUNT=4 THEN MODE=128:RETURN
5799  GOSUB 6010:RETURN
5800  REM DO ABSOLUTE OR ZERO PAGE HEX
5805  IF COUNT=2 THEN MODE=4:RETURN
```

```
5810    IF COUNT=4 THEN MODE=32:RETURN
5815    GOSUB 6010:RETURN
6000    REM PRINT ERROR MESSAGES
6005    PRINT "ILLEGAL▲INDIRECT▲INSTRUCTION":ERR=1:RETURN
6010    PRINT "ILLEGAL▲HEXIDECIMAL▲VALUE":ERR=1:RETURN
6020    PRINT "BRANCH▲OUT▲OF▲RANGE":ERR=1:RETURN
6030    PRINT "ILLEGAL▲ADDRESSING▲MODE▲WITH▲INSTRUCTION":ERR=1:RET
        URN
6070    PRINT "ILLEGAL▲OPERAND":ERR=1:RETURN
6080    PRINT "MULTIPLY▲DEFINED▲LABEL":ERR=1:RETURN
6085    PRINT "UNKNOWN▲SYMBOL":ERR=1:RETURN
6418    IF COUNT<>4 THEN GOSUB 6010:RETURN
6500    REM
6505    CH$=""
6510    IF CC>LE THEN RETURN
6515    CH$=LINE$(CC,CC):CC=CC+1:RETURN
6600    REM CHECK IF LABEL IN SYMBOL TABLE AND IF NOT ADD TO IT
6601    LSIZE=SYSL:LABEL$=SYS$:GOSUB 6700:IF FOUND=1 THEN GOSUB 60
        80:RETURN
6605    SYMBOL$(EPOIN,EPOIN)=CHR$(SYSL):EPOIN=EPOIN+1
6610    COUNT=1
6615    FOR I=EPOIN TO EPOIN+SYSL-1
6617    SYMBOL$(I,I)=SYS$(COUNT,COUNT)
6618    COUNT=COUNT+1:NEXT I
6620    EPOIN=EPOIN+SYSL:SYMBOL$(EPOIN,EPOIN)=CHR$(V):EPOIN=EPOIN+
        1
6622    MSB=INT(PG/256):LSB=PG-(MSB*256)
6624    SYMBOL$(EPOIN,EPOIN)=CHR$(LSB):EPOIN=EPOIN+1
6626    SYMBOL$(EPOIN,EPOIN)=CHR$(MSB):EPOIN=EPOIN+1:SYMBOL$(EPOIN
        ,EPOIN)=CHR$(0):RETURN
6700    REM SEARCH SYMBOL TABLE
6701    SPOIN=1:FOUND=0
6705    A$=SYMBOL$(SPOIN,SPOIN):A=ASC(A$):IF A=0 THEN RETURN
6710    IF A<>LSIZE THEN SPOIN=SPOIN+A+4:GOTO 6705
6715    SA=SPOIN:SPOIN=SPOIN+1:COUNT=1
6720    FOR I=SPOIN TO SPOIN+A-1
6725    IF LABEL$(COUNT,COUNT)<>SYMBOL$(I,I) THEN SPOIN=SA+A+4:GOT
        O 6705
6730    COUNT=COUNT+1:NEXT I
6735    SPOIN=SA+A+1:FOUND=1:LSI=ASC(SYMBOL$(SPOIN,SPOIN))
6740    IF LSI=2 THEN GOSUB 6770:COUNT=4:RETURN
6745    IF LSI=1 THEN GOSUB 6780:COUNT=2:RETURN
6750    RETURN
6770    SPOIN=SPOIN+1:BYTE=ASC(SYMBOL$(SPOIN,SPOIN)):PM=BYTE:GOSUB
        9200:LVALUE$(3,4)=HX$
6775    SPOIN=SPOIN+1:BYTE=ASC(SYMBOL$(SPOIN,SPOIN)):PM=PM+(BYTE*2
        56):GOSUB 9200:LVALUE$(1,2)=HX$:RETURN
6780    SPOIN=SPOIN+1:BYTE=ASC(SYMBOL$(SPOIN,SPOIN)):PM=BYTE:GOSUB
        9200:LVALUE$(1,2)=HX$:RETURN
6800    REM GET CHAR FROM OPERAND
6805    TR=0:CH$=""
6810    IF CC>OP THEN RETURN
6815    CH$=OPER$(CC,CC):CC=CC+1:A=ASC(CH$)
6820    IF A>=65 AND A<=90 THEN TR=1:RETURN
6825    RETURN
7000    REM GENERATE OBJECT CODE
7001    IF ERR=1 THEN RETURN
7002    IF TYPE=2 THEN RETURN
7005    ADDR=ASC(INFOS$(4,4))+(ASC(INFOS$(5,5))*256)
7010    A=USR(ADR(MAND$),ADDR,MODE):IF A=0 THEN GOSUB 6030:RETURN
```

```
7015    COUNT=0
7020    FOR I=0 TO NMODE
7025    A=USR(ADR(MAND$),ADDR,2^I):IF A<>0 THEN COUNT=COUNT+1
7030    A=USR(ADR(MAND$),MODE,2^I):IF A<>0 THEN GOTO 7040
7035    NEXT I
7040    OBJECT=ASC(INFOS$(5+COUNT,5+COUNT))
7045    IF MODE=1 THEN GOSUB 8050:RETURN
7050    IF MODE=2 THEN GOSUB 8100:RETURN
7055    IF MODE=4 THEN GOSUB 8150:RETURN
7060    IF MODE=8 THEN GOSUB 8150:RETURN
7065    IF MODE=16 THEN GOSUB 8150:RETURN
7070    IF MODE=32 THEN GOSUB 8300:RETURN
7075    IF MODE=64 THEN GOSUB 8300:RETURN
7080    IF MODE=128 THEN GOSUB 8300:RETURN
7085    IF MODE=256 THEN GOSUB 8500:RETURN
7090    IF MODE=512 THEN GOSUB 8500:RETURN
7095    IF MODE=1024 THEN GOSUB 8300:RETURN
7099    IF MODE=2048 THEN GOSUB 8600:RETURN
7499    RETURN
7500    REM PRINT OUT THE LINE
7501    IF ERR=1 THEN RETURN
7505    PRINT PU$:RETURN
7600    REM PRINT OUT SYMBOL TABLE
7602    PRINT :PRINT "SYMBOL▲TABLE"
7605    SPOIN=1
7610    A$=SYMBOL$(SPOIN,SPOIN):A=ASC(A$):IF A=0 THEN RETURN
7615    SPOIN=SPOIN+1:LABEL$="▲▲▲▲▲▲▲▲▲▲":CO=1
7620    FOR I=SPOIN TO SPOIN+A-1
7625    LABEL$(CO,CO)=SYMBOL$(I,I):CO=CO+1
7630    NEXT I
7635    SPOIN=SPOIN+A+1
7640    L1=ASC(SYMBOL$(SPOIN,SPOIN)):SPOIN=SPOIN+1
7645    M1=ASC(SYMBOL$(SPOIN,SPOIN)):SPOIN=SPOIN+1
7650    PRINT LABEL$;"▲";
7655    BYTE=M1:GOSUB 9200:PRINT HX$;
7660    BYTE=L1:GOSUB 9200:PRINT HX$:GOTO 7610
8050    REM GENERATE IMPLIED OBJECT
8055    GOSUB 9100:MEM(NC)=OBJECT
8060    NC=NC+1:PC=PC+1
8065    BYTE=OBJECT:GOSUB 9200
8070    PU$(6,7)=HX$:GOSUB 9300:RETURN
8100    REM GENERATE IMMEDIATE OBJ CODE
8105    GOSUB 9100:MEM(NC)=OBJECT
8110    NC=NC+1:MEM(NC)=IMM:NC=NC+1
8115    BYTE=OBJECT:GOSUB 9200:PC=PC+2
8120    PU$(6,7)=HX$:BYTE=IMM:GOSUB 9200
8125    PU$(9,10)=HX$:GOSUB 9300:RETURN
8150    REM GENERATE OBJECT FROM ZERO
8155    GOSUB 9100:MEM(NC)=OBJECT:NC=NC+1
8160    BYTE=OBJECT:GOSUB 9200
8165    PU$(6,7)=HX$:PU$(9,10)=MEM$:NC=NC+1:GOSUB 9300:PC=PC+2:RET
        URN
8300    REM PROCESS ABSOLUTE
8305    GOSUB 9100:MEM(NC)=OBJECT
8310    NC=NC+1:BYTE=OBJECT:GOSUB 9200:PU$(6,7)=HX$
8315    HX$=MEM$(3,4):PU$(9,10)=HX$:GOSUB 9000:MEM(NC)=DEC:NC=NC+1
8317    HX$=MEM$(1,2):PU$(12,13)=HX$:GOSUB 9000:MEM(NC)=DEC:NC=NC+
        1:PC=PC+3
8319    GOSUB 9300:RETURN
8500    REM INDIRECT,Y
8505    GOSUB 9100:MEM(NC)=OBJECT:NC=NC+1
8510    HX$=MEM$(1,2):GOSUB 9000:MEM(NC)=DEC
```

144

```
8515    NC=NC+1:PC=PC+2
8520    BYTE=OBJECT:GOSUB 9200:PU$(6,7)=HX$
8525    PU$(9,10)=MEM$
8530    GOSUB 9300:RETURN
8600    REM RELATIVE BRANCH
8602    IF PAS=1 THEN 8630
8605    HX$=MEM$(1,2):GOSUB 9000:MSB=DEC
8610    HX$=MEM$(3,4):GOSUB 9000:LSB=DEC
8615    LA=(MSB*256)+LSB:DI=LA-PC-2
8620    IF DI>129 THEN GOSUB 6020:RETURN
8625    IF DI<-126 THEN GOSUB 6020:RETURN
8627    IF DI<0 THEN DI=DI+256
8630    GOSUB 9100:MEM(NC)=OBJECT:NC=NC+1
8635    MEM(NC)=DI:NC=NC+1:PC=PC+2
8637    BYTE=DI:GOSUB 9200:PU$(9,10)=HX$
8640    BYTE=OBJECT:GOSUB 9200:PU$(6,7)=HX$
8645    GOSUB 9300:RETURN
9000    REM CONVERT VALUE IN HX$ TO DEC
9005    A$=HX$(1,1):GOSUB 9020
9010    DEC=BYTE*16:A$=HX$(2,2):GOSUB 9020
9015    DEC=DEC+BYTE:RETURN
9020    BYTE=0:IF A$>=CHR$(48) AND A$<=CHR$(57) THEN BYTE=ASC(A$)-
        48:RETURN
9025    IF A$>=CHR$(65) AND A$<=CHR$(70) THEN BYTE=ASC(A$)-55:RETU
        RN
9030    GOSUB 6010:RETURN
9100    REM CONVERT PC TO HEX
9105    M1=INT(PC/256):BYTE=M1:GOSUB 9200:PU$(1,2)=HX$:L1=PC-(M1*2
        56):BYTE=L1:GOSUB 9200:PU$(3,4)=HX$:RETURN
9200    REM CONVERT BYTE TO HX$
9205    MSB=INT(BYTE/16):LSB=BYTE-(MSB*16)
9210    HX$(1,1)=H$(MSB+1,MSB+1):HX$(2,2)=H$(LSB+1,LSB+1):RETURN
9300    REM PUT OPERATION
9305    IF SYSL<>0 THEN PU$(15,15+SYSL-1)=SYS$
9307    PU$(23,25)=CODE$
9310    PU$(28,28+LEN(OPER$))=OPER$
9315    RETURN
9500    REM DATA FOR ASSEMBLER
9505    DATA 56
9507    DATA ADC,1006,8,105,101,117,109,125,121,113,97
9509    DATA AND,1006,8,41,37,53,45,61,57,49,33
9511    DATA ASL,109,5,10,06,22,14,30
9513    DATA BCC,2048,1,144
9515    DATA BCS,2048,1,176
9517    DATA BEQ,2048,1,240
9519    DATA BIT,36,2,36,44
9521    DATA BMI,2048,1,48
9523    DATA BNE,2048,1,208
9525    DATA BPL,2048,1,16
9527    DATA BRK,1,1,00
9529    DATA BVC,2048,1,80
9531    DATA BVS,2048,1,112
9533    DATA CLC,1,1,24
9535    DATA CLD,1,1,216
9537    DATA CLI,1,1,88
9539    DATA CLV,1,1,184
9541    DATA CMP,1006,8,201,197,213,205,221,217,209,193
9543    DATA CPX,38,3,224,228,236
9545    DATA CPY,38,3,192,196,204
9547    DATA DEC,108,4,198,214,206,222
9549    DATA DEX,1,1,202
```

```
9551    DATA DEY,1,1,136
9553    DATA EOR,1006,8,73,69,85,77,93,89,81,65
9555    DATA INC,108,4,230,246,238,254
9557    DATA INX,1,1,232
9559    DATA INY,1,1,200
9561    DATA JMP,1056,2,76,108
9563    DATA JSR,32,1,32
9565    DATA LDA,1006,8,169,165,181,173,189,185,177,161
9567    DATA LDX,182,5,162,166,182,174,190
9569    DATA LDY,110,5,160,164,180,172,29
9571    DATA LSR,45,4,74,70,86,78
9573    DATA NOP,1,1,234
9575    DATA ORA,1006,8,9,5,21,13,29,25,17,1
9577    DATA PHA,1,1,72
9579    DATA PHP,1,1,8
9581    DATA PLA,1,1,104
9583    DATA PLP,1,1,40
9585    DATA ROL,109,5,42,38,54,46,62
9587    DATA ROR,109,5,106,102,118,110,126
9589    DATA RTI,1,1,64
9591    DATA RTS,1,1,96
9593    DATA SBC,1006,8,233,229,245,237,253,249,241,225
9595    DATA SEC,1,1,56
9597    DATA SED,1,1,248
9599    DATA SEI,1,1,120
9600    DATA STA,1004,7,133,149,141,157,153,145,129
9602    DATA STX,52,3,134,150,142
9604    DATA STY,44,3,132,148,140
9606    DATA TAX,1,1,170
9608    DATA TAY,1,1,168
9610    DATA TSX,1,1,186
9612    DATA TXA,1,1,138
9614    DATA TXS,1,1,154
9616    DATA TYA,1,1,152
9801    INPUT #1,LINE$:COUNT=LEN(LINE$)+1:RETURN
11000 REM APPEND
11005 PRINT NL;" ▶";:GOSUB 9801
11010 IF COUNT=1 THEN RETURN
11015 JJ=1:COUNT=COUNT-1
11020 ST1(NL)=FR:JJ=1
11025 FOR I=FR TO FR+COUNT-1:TEXT$(I,I)=LINE$(JJ,JJ):JJ=JJ+1:NEX
      T I
11030 EN1(NL)=FR+COUNT-1:FR=FR+COUNT:NL=NL+1:GOTO 11005
11100 REM LIST
11101 IF NL=1 THEN RETURN
11105 INPUT F1,F2
11106 IF F2>=NL THEN F2=NL-1
11110 FOR I=1 TO NL
11115 IF I>=F1 AND I<=F2 THEN GOSUB 11125
11120 NEXT I:RETURN
11125 ST1=ST1(I):EN1=EN1(I)
11130 PRINT I;" ";:FOR J=ST1 TO EN1:PRINT TEXT$(J,J);:NEXT J:PRI
      NT :RETURN
11160 GOTO 11520
11200 REM DELETE
11205 INPUT F1
11210 IF F1>NL-1 OR F1<1 THEN RETURN
11215 IF F1=NL-1 THEN NL=NL-1:RETURN
11220 JJ=F1:F1=F1+1
11225 FOR I=F1 TO NL
11230 EN1=EN1(I):ST1=ST1(I):EN1(JJ)=EN1:ST1(JJ)=ST1:JJ=JJ+1:NEXT
      I:NL=NL-1:RETURN
```

```
11300 REM INSERT
11305 INPUT F1
11306 IF·F1>=NL THEN RETURN
11310 F1=F1+1
11315 PRINT F1;" ▶";:GOSUB 9801
11325 IF COUNT=1 THEN RETURN
11330 COUNT=COUNT-1:ST1=FR:JJ=1
11335 FOR I=FR TO FR+COUNT-1:TEXT$(I,I)=LINE$(JJ,JJ):JJ=JJ+1:NEX
      T I
11340 EN1=FR+COUNT-1
11345 J=NL-F1:SO=NL-1:LINK=NL
11350 FOR I=1 TO J
11355 A=ST1(SO):ST1(LINK)=A:A=EN1(SO):EN1(LINK)=A:SO=SO-1:LINK=L
      INK-1:NEXT I
11360 EN1(F1)=EN1:ST1(F1)=ST1:FR=FR+COUNT:NL=NL+1:GOTO 11310
11400 REM SAVE
11405 IF NL=1 THEN RETURN
11407 OPER$="":INPUT OPER$:IF OPER$="" THEN RETURN
11410 OPEN #2,8,0,OPER$:A$=" ."
11415 FOR I=1 TO NL-1
11420 EN1=EN1(I):ST1=ST1(I)
11425 FOR J=ST1 TO EN1:A$=TEXT$(J,J)
11430 PRINT #2;A$:PRINT A$;
11450 NEXT J
11455 PRINT #2;" ⊢":PRINT
11460 NEXT I:CLOSE #2:RETURN
11500 REM LOAD
11505 OPER$="":INPUT OPER$:IF OPER$="" THEN RETURN
11510 OPEN #2,4,0,OPER$
11512 TRAP 11570
11515 FR=1:ST1=FR:I=1
11520 ST1=FR:COUNT=1:LINE$=" ▲▲▲▲▲▲▲▲▲▲▲▲▲▲▲▲▲▲▲▲▲▲"
11525 A$=" .":INPUT #2;A$:IF A$=" ⊢" THEN PRINT :GOTO 11540
11530 LINE$(COUNT,COUNT)=A$:PRINT A$;
11535 COUNT=COUNT+1:GOTO 11525
11540 COUNT=COUNT-1
11545 EN1=FR+COUNT-1
11550 JJ=1:FOR J=FR TO FR+COUNT-1:TEXT$(J,J)=LINE$(JJ,JJ):JJ=JJ+
      1:NEXT J
11555 ST1(I)=ST1:EN1(I)=EN1:I=I+1:FR=FR+COUNT
11560 GOTO 11520
11570 NL=I:CLOSE #2:RETURN
12000 REM COMMAND MODE
12005 CLOSE #1:OPEN #1,12,0,"E:"
12006 SETCOLOR 1,0,15:SETCOLOR 4,0,0:SETCOLOR 2,0,0:POKE 82,0:PR
      INT
12007 POKE 676,16:POKE 675,8:POKE 677,16
12010 LINE$=" .":PRINT "* .";:GOSUB 9801
12020 IF LINE$="ASM" THEN GOSUB 20:GOTO 12010
12030 IF LINE$="APPEND" THEN GOSUB 11000:GOTO 12010
12040 IF LINE$="LIST" THEN GOSUB 11100:GOTO 12010
12050 IF LINE$="WATCH" THEN GOSUB 13000:GOTO 12010
12055 IF·LINE$="NWATCH" THEN WA=0:GOTO 12010
12060 IF LINE$="QUIT" THEN PRINT CHR$(125);:END
12065 IF LINE$="NEW" THEN FR=1:NL=1:GOTO 12010
12070 IF LINE$="DELETE" THEN GOSUB 11200:GOTO 12010
12075 IF LINE$="INSERT" THEN GOSUB 11300:GOTO 12010
12080 IF LINE$="RUN" THEN GOSUB 13500:GOTO 12010
12085 IF LINE$="SAVE" THEN GOSUB 11400:GOTO 12010
12087 IF LINE$="LOAD" THEN GOSUB 11500:GOTO 12010
12099 GOTO 12010
```

```
13000 REM WATCH
13010 PRINT "(WHAT ADDRESS )";
13015 INPUT HZ$
13020 IF LEN(HZ$)<>4 THEN PRINT "ADDRESS MUST BE FOUR DIGITS LON
      G":RETURN
13030 HX$=HZ$(1,2):GOSUB 9000:M1=DEC
13035 HX$=HZ$(3,4):GOSUB 9000:L1=DEC
13040 WAT=(M1*256)+L1:WA=1:RETURN
13500 REM RUN
13510 JJ=PC1
13515 FOR I=1 TO NC-1:BYTE=MEM(I):POKE JJ,BYTE:JJ=JJ+1:NEXT I
13520 IF WA=1 THEN BYTE=PEEK(WAT):GOSUB 9200:PRINT "ADDRESS ";HZ
      $;" BEFORE=";HX$
13530 A=USR(PC1)
13540 IF WA=1 THEN BYTE=PEEK(WAT):GOSUB 9200:PRINT "ADDRESS ";HZ
      $;" AFTER =";HX$
13550 RETURN
```

148

```
1000    ? CHR$(125):? :? :? :? :? "ENTER ᴧCMD ᴧFOR ᴧCOMMAND ᴧSUMMARY":? :
        ?
1010    DIM CMD$(50)
1020    DIM WHAT$(3)
1030    DIM TEST$(3)
1040    DIM HEX$(16):HEX$="0123456789ABCDEF"
1050    DIM TEMP$(30)
1060    DIM T$(30)
1070    DIM OP$(3)
1080    DIM FIELD$(10)
1900    LOCATION=1536
2000    ? :? CHR$(20);::INPUT CMD$
2010    IF LEN(CMD$)<3 THEN GOSUB 5000:GOTO 2000
2020    WHAT$=CMD$(1,3)
2030    RESTORE 3000
2040    READ TEST$,WHERE
2050    IF TEST$="XXX" THEN CMD$="":GOTO 2010
2060    IF TEST$=WHAT$ THEN GOTO WHERE
2070    GOTO 2040
2100    ? :? :? "COMMANDS ARE":? :?
2110    RESTORE 3000
2120    READ TEST$,WHERE
2130    IF TEST$="XXX" THEN ? :? :GOTO 2000
2140    ? TEST$
2150    GOTO 2120
3000    DATA EXI,3100
3003    DATA DUM,3300
3004    DATA MEM,6300
3005    DATA ASC,3400
3006    DATA CMD,2100
3098    DATA XXX,2000
3100    ? :? :? "TO ᴧRESTART":? "TYPE ᴧᴧᴧᴧGOTO ᴧ2000 ᴧ[RETURN]":? :?
        :END
3300    ? :? "START ᴧDUMP ᴧAT ᴧ$";:INPUT TEMP$:GOSUB 4500:IF ERRORFLA
        G THEN GOSUB 5001:? :GOTO 2000
3305    DUMP=TEMP
3310    FOR Y=1 TO 22:TEMP=DUMP:GOSUB 4000:? "$";TEMP$;" ᴧᴧ";
3320    FOR XX=1 TO 10:TEMP=PEEK(DUMP):GOSUB 3350:GOSUB 4000:? TEM
        P$(3,4);" ᴧ";:NEXT XX:? :NEXT Y:? :? "?";
3330    INPUT TEMP$:IF TEMP$="E" THEN 2000
3340    GOTO 3310
3350    DUMP=DUMP+1:IF DUMP>65535 THEN DUMP=DUMP-65536
3360    RETURN
3400    ? "START ᴧADDRESS ᴧFOR ᴧASCII ᴧDUMP ᴧ$";:INPUT. TEMP$:GOSUB 4500
        :IF ERRORFLAG THEN GOSUB 5001:? :GOTO 2000
3410    DUMP=TEMP
3420    FOR Y=1 TO 22:TEMP=DUMP:GOSUB 4000:? "$";TEMP$;" ᴧᴧ";
3430    FOR XX=1 TO 30:TEMP=PEEK(DUMP):DUMP=DUMP+1:IF TEMP>122 OR
        TEMP<32 THEN TEMP=ASC(".")
3440    ? CHR$(TEMP);:IF DUMP>65535 THEN DUMP=DUMP-65535
3450    NEXT XX:? :NEXT Y
3460    ? "?";:INPUT TEMP$:IF TEMP$="E" THEN 2000
3470    GOTO 3420
4000    TEMP$=" ᴧᴧᴧᴧ":X=INT(TEMP/4096)
4010    TEMP$(1,1)=HEX$(X+1,X+1)
4020    TEMP=TEMP-X*4096:X=INT(TEMP/256)
4030    TEMP$(2,2)=HEX$(X+1,X+1)
4040    TEMP=TEMP-X*256:X=INT(TEMP/16)
```

149

```
4050    TEMP$(3,3)=HEX$(X+1,X+1)
4060    TEMP=TEMP-X*16:X=TEMP
4070    TEMP$(4,4)=HEX$(X+1,X+1):RETURN
4500    ERRORFLAG=0:IF LEN(TEMP$)>4 THEN ERRORFLAG=1:RETURN
4510    TEMP=0:MULT=1:FOR X=LEN(TEMP$) TO 1 STEP -1
4520    T$=TEMP$(X,X):IF T$>="0" AND T$<="9" THEN TEMP=TEMP+VAL(T$
        )*MULT:GOTO 4600
4530    IF T$<"A" OR T$>"F" THEN ERRORFLAG=1
4540    TEMP=TEMP+((ASC(T$)-55)*MULT)
4600    MULT=MULT*16:NEXT X:RETURN
5000    ? "Syntax error";:RETURN
5001    ? "Not valid hex";:RETURN
6000    DATA BRK,10,0          6050    DATA X,10,0
6001    DATA ORA,8,1           6051    DATA X,10,0
6002    DATA X,10,0            6052    DATA X,10,0
6003    DATA X,10,0            6053    DATA AND,4,1
6004    DATA X,10,0            6054    DATA ROL,4,1
6005    DATA ORA,1,1           6055    DATA X,10,0
6006    DATA ASL,1,1           6056    DATA SEC,10,0
6007    DATA X,10,0            6057    DATA AND,12,2
6008    DATA PHP,10,0          6058    DATA X,10,0
6009    DATA ORA,7,1           6059    DATA X,10,0
6010    DATA ASL,13,0          6060    DATA X,10,0
6011    DATA X,10,0            6061    DATA AND,11,2
6012    DATA X,10,0            6062    DATA ROL,11,2
6013    DATA ORA,2,2           6063    DATA X,10,0
6014    DATA ASL,2,2           6064    DATA RTI,10,0
6015    DATA X,10,0            6065    DATA EOR,8,1
6016    DATA BPL,3,1           6066    DATA X,10,0
6017    DATA ORA,9,1           6067    DATA X,10,0
6018    DATA X,10,0            6068    DATA X,10,0
6019    DATA X,10,0            6069    DATA EOR,1,1
6020    DATA X,10,0            6070    DATA LSR,1,1
6021    DATA ORA,4,1           6071    DATA X,10,0
6022    DATA ASL,4,1           6072    DATA PHA,10,0
6023    DATA X,10,0            6073    DATA EOR,7,1
6024    DATA CLC,10,0          6074    DATA LSR,13,0
6025    DATA ORA,12,2          6075    DATA X,10,0
6026    DATA X,10,0            6076    DATA JMP,0,2
6027    DATA X,10,0            6077    DATA EOR,2,2
6028    DATA X,10,0            6078    DATA LSR,2,2
6029    DATA ORA,11,2          6079    DATA X,10,0
6030    DATA ASL,11,2          6080    DATA BVC,3,1
6031    DATA X,10,0            6081    DATA EOR,9,1
6032    DATA JSR,0,2           6082    DATA X,10,0
6033    DATA AND,8,1           6083    DATA X,10,0
6034    DATA X,10,0            6084    DATA X,10,0
6035    DATA X,10,0            6085    DATA EOR,4,1
6036    DATA BIT,1,1           6086    DATA LSR,4,1
6037    DATA AND,1,1           6087    DATA X,10,0
6038    DATA ROL,1,1           6088    DATA CLI,10,0
6039    DATA X,10,0            6089    DATA EOR,12,2
6040    DATA PLP,10,0          6090    DATA X,10,0
6041    DATA AND,7,1           6091    DATA X,10,0
6042    DATA ROL,13,0          6092    DATA X,10,0
6043    DATA X,10,0            6093    DATA EOR ,11,2
6044    DATA BIT,2,2           6094    DATA LSR,11,2
6045    DATA AND,2,2           6095    DATA X,10,0
6046    DATA ROL,2,2           6096    DATA RTS,10,0
6047    DATA X,10,0            6097    DATA ADC,8,1
6048    DATA BMI,3,1           6098    DATA X,10,0
6049    DATA AND,9,1           6099    DATA X,10,0
```

150

```
6100    DATA X,10,0              6161    DATA LDA,8,1
6101    DATA ADC,1,1             6162    DATA LDX,7,1
6102    DATA ROR,1,1             6163    DATA X,10,0
6103    DATA X,10,0              6164    DATA LDY,1,1
6104    DATA PLA,10,0            6165    DATA LDA,1,1
6105    DATA ADC,7,1             6166    DATA LDX,1,1
6106    DATA ROR,13,0            6167    DATA X,10,0
6107    DATA X,10,0              6168    DATA TAY,10,0
6108    DATA JMP,6,2             6169    DATA LDA,7,1
6109    DATA ADC,2,2             6170    DATA TAX,10,0
6110    DATA ROR,2,2             6171    DATA X,10,0
6111    DATA X,10,0              6172    DATA LDY,2,2
6112    DATA BVS,3,1             6173    DATA LDA,2,2
6113    DATA ADC,9,1             6174    DATA LDX,2,2
6114    DATA X,10,0              6175    DATA X,10,0
6115    DATA X,10,0              6176    DATA BCS,3,1
6116    DATA X,10,0              6177    DATA LDA,9,1
6117    DATA ADC,4,1             6178    DATA X,10,0
6118    DATA ROR ,4,1            6179    DATA X,10,0
6119    DATA X,10,0              6180    DATA LDY,4,1
6120    DATA SEI,10,0            6181    DATA LDA,4,1
6121    DATA ADC,12,2            6182    DATA LDX,5,1
6122    DATA X,10,0              6183    DATA X,10,0
6123    DATA X,10,0              6184    DATA CLV,10,0
6124    DATA X,10,0              6185    DATA LDA,12,2
6125    DATA ADC,11,2            6186    DATA TSX,10,0
6126    DATA ROR,11,2            6187    DATA X,10,0
6127    DATA X,10,0              6188    DATA LDY,11,2
6128    DATA X,10,0              6189    DATA LDA,11,2
6129    DATA STA,8,1             6190    DATA LDX,12,2
6130    DATA X,10,0              6191    DATA X,10,0
6131    DATA X,10,0              6192    DATA CPY,7,1
6132    DATA STY,1,1             6193    DATA CMP,8,1
6133    DATA STA,1,1             6194    DATA X,10,0
6134    DATA STX,1,1             6195    DATA X,10,0
6135    DATA X,10,0              6196    DATA CPY,1,1
6136    DATA DEY,10,0            6197    DATA CMP,1,1
6137    DATA X,10,0              6198    DATA DEC,1,1
6138    DATA TXA,10,0            6199    DATA X,10,0
6139    DATA X,10,0              6200    DATA INY,10,0
6140    DATA STY,2,2             6201    DATA CMP,7,1
6141    DATA STA,2,2             6202    DATA DEX,10,0
6142    DATA STX,2,2             6203    DATA X,10,0
6143    DATA X,10,0              6204    DATA CPY,2,2
6144    DATA BCC,3,1             6205    DATA CMP,2,2
6145    DATA STA,9,1             6206    DATA DEC,2,2
6146    DATA X,10,0              6207    DATA X,10,0
6147    DATA X,10,0              6208    DATA BNE,3,1
6148    DATA STY,4,1             6209    DATA CMP,9,1
6149    DATA STA,4,1             6210    DATA X,10,0
6150    DATA STX,5,1             6211    DATA X,10,0
6151    DATA X,10,0              6212    DATA X,10,0
6152    DATA TYA,10,0            6213    DATA CMP,4,1
6153    DATA STA,12,2            6214    DATA DEC,4,1
6154    DATA TXS,10,0            6215    DATA X,10,0
6155    DATA X,10,0              6216    DATA CLD,10,0
6156    DATA X,10,0              6217    DATA CMP,12,2
6157    DATA STA,11,2            6218    DATA X,10,0
6158    DATA X,10,0              6219    DATA X,10,0
6159    DATA X,10,0              6220    DATA X,10,0
6160    DATA LDY,7,1             6221    DATA CMP,11,2
```

```
6222    DATA DEC,11,2                    6239    DATA X,10,0
6223    DATA X,10,0                      6240    DATA BEQ,3,1
6224    DATA CPX,7,1                     6241    DATA SBC,9,1
6225    DATA SBC,8,1                     6242    DATA X,10,0
6226    DATA X,10,0                      6243    DATA X,10,0
6227    DATA X,10,0                      6244    DATA X,10,0
6228    DATA CPX,1,1                     6245    DATA SBC,4,1
6229    DATA SBC,1,1                     6246    DATA INC,4,1
6230    DATA INC,1,1                     6247    DATA X,10,0
6231    DATA X,10,0                      6248    DATA SED,10,0
6232    DATA INX,10,0                    6249    DATA SBC,12,2
6233    DATA SBC,7,1                     6250    DATA X,10,0
6234    DATA NOP,10,0                    6251    DATA X,10,0
6235    DATA X,10,0                      6252    DATA X,10,0
6236    DATA CPX,2,2                     6253    DATA SBC,11,2
6237    DATA SBC,2,2                     6254    DATA INC,11,2
6238    DATA INC,2,2                     6255    DATA X,10,0


6300    ? :? "START ▲ADDRESS▲$";:INPUT TEMP$
6310    GOSUB 4500:IF ERRORFLAG THEN GOSUB 5001:? :GOTO 2000
6320    PC=TEMP
6400    FOR Y=1 TO 22
6410    WHERE=PEEK(PC)+6000:RESTORE WHERE
6420    READ OP$,FIELD,BYTES
6430    TEMP=PC:GOSUB 4000:? "$";TEMP$;"▲";
6431    IF BYTES=0 THEN TEMP=PEEK(PC):GOSUB 4000:? TEMP$(3,4);"▲▲▲
        ▲▲";:GOTO 6440
6432    IF BYTES=1 THEN TEMP=256*PEEK(PC)+PEEK(PC+1-((PC+1>65535)*
        65536)):GOSUB 4000:? TEMP$;"▲▲▲";:GOTO 6440
6436    TEMP=PEEK(PC):GOSUB 4000:? TEMP$(3,4);:TEMP=PEEK(PC+1-((PC
        +1>65535)*65536)):GOSUB 4000:? TEMP$(3,4);
6437    TEMP=PEEK(PC+2-((PC+2>65535)*65536)):GOSUB 4000
6439    ? TEMP$(3,4);"▲";
6440    PC=PC+1:IF PC>65535 THEN PC=PC-65536
6450    IF OP$="X" THEN ? "???▲":GOTO 6800
6460    ? OP$;"▲▲▲▲";
6470    RESTORE 8000+FIELD
6480    READ FIELD$,START,REP:IF REP THEN FIELD$(REP,REP)=","
6490    IF START=0 THEN ? FIELD$:GOTO 6800
6500    IF BYTES=1 THEN TEMP=PEEK(PC):PC=PC+1:IF PC>65535 THEN PC=
        PC-65535
6510    IF BYTES=2 THEN TEMP=PEEK(PC)+256*PEEK(PC+1):PC=PC+2:IF PC
        >65535 THEN PC=PC-65535
6512    IF FIELD<>3 THEN 6520
6513    IF TEMP>127 THEN TEMP=(TEMP-256)
6514    TEMP=PC+TEMP
6520    GOSUB 4000:IF BYTES=1 AND FIELD<>3 THEN TEMP$=TEMP$(3,4)
6530    FIELD$(START,START+LEN(TEMP$)-1)=TEMP$
6540    ? FIELD$
6800    NEXT Y
6810    ? "?";:INPUT TEMP$:IF TEMP$="E" THEN GOTO 2000
6820    GOTO 6400
8000    DATA $    ,2,0                   8007    DATA #$   ,3,0
8001    DATA $    ,2,0                   8008    DATA ($ *X),3,5
8002    DATA $    ,2,0                   8009    DATA ($ )*Y,3,6
8003    DATA $    ,2,0                   8010    DATA ,0,0
8004    DATA $ *X,2,4                    8011    DATA $    *X,2,6
8005    DATA $ *Y,2,4                    8012    DATA $    *Y,2,6
8006    DATA ($   ),3,0                  8013    DATA A,0,0
```

Index